Same Sh*t.

Different Date.

Same Sh*t.
Different Date.

Why You Keep Attracting the Same Wrong
Partners – and How to Finally Solve It!

Dave Elliott

This book is dedicated to
my beloved wife, Katrina.

The following are trademarks belonging exclusively to Dave Elliott and
Legendary Love Publishing Company, a division of MPower Unlimited,
Incorporated:
R.O.O.T.; C.O.R.E.; H.E.A.R.T.; H.E.A.R.T. Flips; Legendary Love for
Life; 12 Traumatic M.I.S.B.E.H.A.V.I.O.R.S.;
The 8 F's of Personal Transformation

Table of Contents

Dedication: pg. 11

Acknowledgements: pg. 13

Chapter 1: pg. 17
The Hidden Gifts in Your Relationships

Chapter 2: pg. 25
Getting Down to the R.O.O.T. of the C.O.R.E.

Chapter 3: pg. 35
Here We Go Again...
or Why the Hell Does this Keep Happening?!?

Chapter 4: pg. 40
Soul Mate or Soul Messenger?

Chapter 5: pg. 51
Magical Morphing Messengers

Chapter 6: pg. 59
"My Ex Did a Number on Me."
How to Identify Recurring Patterns

Chapter 7: pg. 77
Uncover Your Soul Messenger Matrix:
Freedom Awaits in Your H.E.A.R.T.™

Chapter 8: pg. 89
Into the Matrix - Revealed:
New Awareness for Old Issues

Chapter 9: pg. 133
The ABC's of Healing

Chapter 10: pg. 158
Same Old Story, Brand New Happy Ending

Chapter 11: pg. 191
Knowing and Showing Your Value:
The 8 F's of Personal Transformation

Chapter 12: pg. 212
Growing Your Greatness:
The 8 F's of Personal Transformation

Chapter 13: pg. 226
The Past May Predict Your Future
but It's not Predetermined

Appendix: pg. 233

About the Author: pg. 243

Dedication

For me, the process of writing a book is a labor of love. It is also a labor for love, about love and for the purpose of creating even more love in the world. I dedicate this book to my dear wife, Katrina, for without her, this, my second book, would not be possible.

One of the ideas I share in the book is about the ever-present concept of support and challenge, and my dear wife provides me with plenty of both. When it comes to support, Katrina inspires me daily and supports our team as we live our mission to travel the world together to touch, move and inspire others in the area of relationship. It is also her selfless-sacrifice that allows me the freedom to pursue such a time and labor-intensive process as writing a book. Her patience, tolerance and willingness to be flexible are invaluable to me. It does cut into our time together, but it is her willingness to look after me while immersed in writing that allows me to serve and look after the people who will read and benefit from this book.

In addition, when it comes to challenge, she has been instrumental in helping me discover and work on healing my own shadow so that I can help *you* do the same for yours, both through this very book and in my one-on-one coaching. Her perspective has helped me see my own, unresolved areas that would have remained hidden away, out of sight and mind, had they not been illuminated by the interactions between us. Her combination of speaking her truth with candor and compassion is the embodiment of unconditional love. In addition, her patience has helped me eventually see what she means even when I'm not yet ready or able to receive the learning.

It is exactly this kind of unconditional love, mixed with support and challenge, that I wish for you so that you can do your own healing work. While some may want to pass on the challenge part, you certainly can't heal what you don't see or feel, so having a loving and patient partner to help reveal those things to you is an invaluable gift from the universe. I urge you to learn from this book and my own example in order to welcome the reflection you see of yourself in your partner's eyes. Even though it may not always feel good in the moment, it is a gift when you find the lesson and resolve it. For good.

Lastly, I hope that if this book serves you or moves you in any way, and if you ever have the opportunity, you will thank my wife for her contribution and sacrifice just as you might thank me.

Acknowledgments

As I celebrate the completion of my second book, I have to start by thanking and acknowledging some of the top names in the fields of relationship and personal development who came before me. It was their groundbreaking ideas and body of work that inspired my own thinking and creativity and the result is this book.

The central theme of this book is based on the underpinnings of a concept known as Imago Therapy, which was developed by best-selling authors Harville Hendrix, Ph.D. and Helen LaKelly Hunt, Ph.D. They used the Latin word Imago, meaning *image*, because it described the process of molding that helps shape children in their formative years. This process of influencing the behavior of children creates their world view and forms the basis of their beliefs, expectations, self-esteem, habits and more. While the Imago process, as it was conceived, is heavily based on communication models and methods that lead to healing between adult couples, I have developed and adapted some other strategies that help heal those underlying, unresolved wounds, especially for singles who are not yet in a relationship but aspire to have one. Those wounds are often out of sight and out of mind and can last well into adulthood, especially when they are conditioned and reinforced over time. In fact, I was inspired to write this book because the simple premise that proactively discovering your own invisible wounds *before* they sabotage relationships is a huge advantage which can save a great deal of pain. It has also given me immense satisfaction on the other side of doing this exact work for myself and I know you can experience that as well.

Another key concept of this book was inspired by a mentor whom I also acknowledged in my first book. John DeMartini is a modern-day genius who applies his wisdom gleaned from a lifetime of studying the best of the best. I first saw him in the groundbreaking movie, *The Secret,* where he caught my attention by sharing some profound information. I first met him when my wife, Katrina, introduced us because she had served as an assistant on one of his speaking tours. He also travels the world non-stop in order to teach his wisdom to others and in the process, changing the world for the better every single day. In John DeMartini's Breakthrough Experience, which I highly recommend, he taught me how to collapse what didn't serve me, honor my value and speak my truth.

John also taught me something that will benefit you directly and greatly in this book. He taught a concept that helps organize a life well-lived into a number of key categories and shows how to reclaim your own value and self-worth in those areas that may require some attention. In my own effort to constantly improve and simplify various personal development methodologies, I created a spin on this which I introduce in Chapter 11 and I call it the 8 F's of Personal Transformation. You may not recognize it based on the way John teaches it, but it is rooted in what he taught, and I believe in acknowledging those who've inspired me. I also mention John fondly in Chapter 4 when I reference some of his teachings on the process of equilibration and not objectifying people by placing them or pedestals or pits. The man has made a profound difference in my life and by sharing some of the things I've learned, I sincerely hope you'll experience a similar shift in your thinking and quality of life.

In addition, I also want to acknowledge, Tony Robbins. As a graduate of his Coaching Academy and a Senior Leader in his organization since 2007, I am extremely grateful for his teachings and influence. I'm grateful to Mr. Robbins for giving me the tools I've used to create massive change for myself, my amazing clients and my dear readers. I've been self-employed and able to serve countless clients around the world for for more than a decade. He not only helped me create a very satisfying life, he also introduced me to my Senior Leader global family of choice and my beloved wife. Indeed, some of my greatest blessings have been a product of my association with the Anthony Robbins organization.

After my role models and teachers who taught and inspired me, there would, likewise, be no book to share without the talents and efforts of my book production team. I'm incredibly grateful for my editor, Julie Keywell, whose eye for detail, knowledge and commitment have been such a gift to me for years. Even more precious to me has been her loyalty, kindness and unwavering support. Once Julie worked her magic with my draft, my other long-time friend and author's consultant, Heather Shreve, took over. With her artist's eye and passion for the written word, her design skill makes me look good. If you've ever enjoyed my writing in book form, you should thank Heather because it was her prolific experience in writing, not to mention her encouragement, that provided the inspiration for me to commit to the writing process. She even named my first book, so she really has been indispensable.

Lastly, I want to thank my amazing clients whose courage and commitment to do the work inspires me daily. I am so blessed to get to live vicariously through their wins, big and small, and I can't even conceive of a more fulfilling way to make my living, or even make a life, for that matter. I truly am blessed to get to do what I do every day and I humbly thank you for your faith, your referrals and your friendship.

It's my sincere hope that the information in this book helps you find a love that heals your old wounds, makes you an even better person than you already are and is real, lasting and deeply fulfilling. In other words, I hope it serves you in finding your very own Legendary Love For Life.

Chapter 1:

The Hidden Gifts
in Your Relationships

 Let's get this out right up front: there's a *very* good chance that up until this moment right now, all of your most intimate relationships have come bearing hidden gifts you didn't recognize or never saw coming. In fact, they're often so stealthy that most people don't even see them months, years, decades – or even a lifetime – later. Now *that's* hidden! Plus, it's also the reason I'm writing this book. I am going to help you change all that right now and save you a great deal of frustration, struggle and pain.

The reason you didn't see these gifts was because without the awareness to know what you're looking for, they hide in plain sight. You see, those hidden gifts are cleverly disguised as problems. Arguments. Disagreements. Fights. Impasses. And yes, even the break-ups, past and present. They're the insidious little idiosyncrasies I also call your secret saboteurs because that they lie in wait and pop up right when you're least expecting them, and least resistant to them, usually when you're under stress. It's kind of like a big tidal wave. If you're not in a great state, with strong physiology, or if you don't see it coming, it just might take you under.

There's More to Attraction than Just Your "Type"

In my presentations and programs, I've asked people what specifically creates attraction between two people. That's usually good for a few laughs when people offer up suggestions like their preferred body parts, interesting fetishes and the usual references from their personal highlight reel of sexy escapades. However, beyond the usual, more human animal-based responses that have to do with physical attraction, there's a host of impulses that are based on human spirit-based attractors which are more emotional in nature or intangible.

In my previous book called *The Catch Your Match Formula™*, I shared a system I developed on how to write effective dating profiles that get results. In that book, I gave some examples of how to describe other types of attractions beyond just the physical in a Chapter I called "Show 'Em Why You're the B.E.S.T." In that Chapter, I focus on the acronym B.E.S.T. to have readers create their profile. First, I get them to outline the Benefits that come from dating them. I suggest they describe the Experience of what it would be like to date or be in relationship with them. Then, I get readers to focus on the Sizzle, excitement or the sex appeal that they aspire to create in their dreams, goals or daily lives.

Finally, I get the reader to feature the Traits they have to offer and communicate them by painting a picture with words and describing scenarios represented by their top traits. Together, these four attributes represent some of the basic building blocks of connection that help bring people together and generate attraction.

But What If That's Not What It Is at All?

This is where I have a bit of a surprise for you. You know that feeling of excitement, or maybe even anxiety, that happens when you feel a "special connection" to someone? You know, the racing pulse, the perspiration, the difficulty swallowing, the inability to speak or think clearly, the inclination to maybe even run away and hide? To some, that may sound like a textbook case of infatuation. Perhaps you never noticed those are the very same physiological symptoms of what is commonly known as the fight or flight response? I'll bet you never thought of it that way because typically, the feeling one gets when you come face-to-face with what could be the love of your life is quite different from the feeling one might get when you have the urge to run from the grave danger of a wild grizzly bear in order to live to tell about it. But as I've just pointed out, the symptoms themselves are identical.

The reason you have that type of response when you are "strangely attracted" to a new potential partner is not because your heart beats as one with this absolute stranger you've just met. In fact, far from it. The reason you feel that response is that something in the connection feels "familiar," as in the word "family." Part of that rush you feel is your soul's recognition that this new person represents some connection to your own unfinished business from childhood. In fact, that bonding you feel may have more to do with the invisible wounds you both have in common, which are so invisible you may not even be aware you have them at all. Or they certainly won't be top-of-mind right there in that moment. But I can assure you, they are there just waiting to be triggered. In fact, no one can trigger a wound like someone who knows that very same wound, intimately.

Sometimes they know only too well what wounded you because they have had similar experiences and seem to be sensitive to them on the surface. However, you will very often attract people on the other side of your issue. The criticized tend to attract criticizers. The abused tend to attract abusers. The rejected or abandoned tend to attract those who are destined to one day reject or abandon. It's almost impossible to chalk that up to happenstance or not see the perfection in those situations when you take a step back and think about it. Let me be clear: I'm not being glib or taking a perverse pleasure in the fact that the abusers and the abused find one another. In fact, I have a great deal of compassion and understanding for both parties, especially the one in the victim role.

When we take a step up and view it from a higher, more enlightened level, you start to realize that *the only thing* that will ever teach someone who's been abused to no longer be the victim is when he or she finally hits threshold and says "no more." When people start to see the *pattern* of abuse they are attracting, it becomes a lot harder to chalk someone else's poor behavior up to the other person rather than finally seeing their own role in that ongoing situation. Let me be very clear, I *am not* victim blaming here. I am not shifting responsibility to the abused or giving abusers a free pass on the damage they cause. Far from it. I am simply pointing out that ALL experiences come to serve, even the painful ones. There is a lesson for the abused and a lesson for the abuser. I'm not saying each party always gets the lesson. I *am* saying that once they *do* get the lesson, new possibilities are created.

Sounds Easy Then, Right?

So, if one knows they have a pattern of attracting all the wrong people, based on their own past history, it should be easy to keep that from happening again, right? Well, maybe, but not so fast. After all, somehow, people who keep attracting unavailable partners find a way to continue that streak. So how do you explain that? Let's not overlook the fact that most people tend to be on their very best behavior when they're trying to impress a new dating interest. In other words, that "best behavior" *specifically* includes hiding the things that we know in advance could pose a problem. Sometimes charming and deceptive are the very same thing. I don't say this to scare you or make you feel hopeless. I say it to explain how very good people, maybe even people just like you, can get pulled into situations they would have ordinarily avoided had they known the whole or complete situation in advance.

Attraction and What You Need to Know

We all know attraction and connection happens at a conscious level when we meet someone who's attractive or who fits our type preference, maybe even someone we just feel good around. We see, hear, feel and know the evidence and that creates the signal that attraction is happening. The point of this book is that I don't want you to overlook that some of what you're feeling as attraction is simultaneously an *unconscious* connection that happens when your wounds and a new person's wounds realize they are compatible or complementary. Humans are influenced by both nature and nurture, so it's not just your DNA or physical attributes in play when you meet someone new. It's also the environment you were raised in and the beliefs you hold, like what you think you deserve or what's way out of your league. Can you see what a huge factor that *one belief* could be between someone you approach and someone you never approach and avoid instead?

While it is often a conscious choice, falling in love is also selection at an unconscious level. In addition to conscious drives like companionship and procreation, we are also unconsciously driven to finish childhood and heal unresolved wounds through our selection of dates or partners. It's about handling our unfinished business and doing what needs to be done.

Once aware of this, we can begin to align your conscious mind with that unconscious agenda and see how it's working *for* you. One of the biggest and most disempowering mistakes we make is assuming that hurts and disappointments are happening *to* us instead of *for* us. Let me be clear: your partner is not there to make you crazy. They are there to help *heal* you and the sooner you get that and adjust your thoughts and behavior accordingly, the sooner you will heal and end any unnecessary suffering.

Another reason to understand this concept is to see the opportunity to grow and heal. If you fail to get the lesson, that only guarantees you will get it again on the next date. It might look much different, but in hindsight, the lesson will be the same or very similar. Of course, it's ultimately your choice. You can either get it now. Or you can get it again.

My hope is that this book will help you stop making your experiences about "them" and start to understand at a deeper level that you always have a role in every situation you co-create. When you make it about what "they" did or said, or didn't do or say, it only ensures that you miss the learning. After all, as the saying goes, it takes two to tango and whether you lead or follow, you still danced.

Let the Conscious Healing Begin!

Conscious healing begins as soon as you stop looking at them and you as separate and start to evaluate your relationship based on the collective "us" or "we." This is when we truly start to see things differently and make the invisible, visible. When we change our thinking, we also start changing our questions and that process inevitably yields all new answers.

Here are a few examples of better-quality questions that lead to more enlightenment and less separation and pain:

Instead of asking "why did they do that?" ask
⇨ **"what was my role in that?"**

Instead of asking "why do they make me feel this way?" ask
⇨ **"what is this triggering in me?"**

Instead of asking "why does this always happen to me" ask
⇨ **"what can I learn from this?"**

Chapter 2:

Getting Down to the R.O.O.T.™ of the C.O.R.E.™

 Now that I've outlined how attraction is really about the sub-consciously guided call to heal unfinished business from childhood wounding, I want to give you a new frame of understanding for what's happening within you and how you find yourself in this position. When you feel strangely attracted to another individual, think of that as your soul's recognition of something you need to get from that person. It's usually an experience or a lesson that will somehow (hopefully) close the loop on an unresolved issue from your past. Now that you are becoming *consciously* awake about what's going on when this happens, the stage is set for what I call a R.O.O.T. Breakthrough.

What is a R.O.O.T. Breakthrough?

Most people struggle in relationships because they have

no idea what the R.O.O.T. cause of the problem *is*, nor do they have the slightest clue about how to fix it. That's about to change forever because I have a new definition that is an absolute game-changer. This simple acronym I've developed will not only lay the groundwork for a brand new and enlightened understanding of an old, unidentified problem, but also define that problem in solvable terms so that it's no longer an invisible saboteur to be feared but instead, a welcome and exciting gateway to new possibilities and hope.

R.O.O.T. Stands for Relationship Origin of Trauma

In order to understand, embrace and resolve this concept, you should know that the root of your struggles is related almost entirely to unconscious wounding that occurred early in your childhood prior to the age of seven years old. That's right. Our very first relationship with our caretakers will lay the groundwork for every relationship we ever have because it was then that you made certain key observations about the world in which you had been born into and now reside. That's why I call this your Origin of Trauma because it's right where it all began. Was it a wonderful world where you were celebrated and had every whim indulged immediately? Was it a world where you were safe, loved and could trust easily? Or was it a world of delayed responses, unanswered cries and indifference? Worse still, was it a world where you felt contempt or even abuse? We now understand that even after these experiences are over or even gone from conscious memory, they are not forgotten. In fact, they are imprinted in the deepest recesses of your brain where survival instincts take root.

A child who is cared for and nurtured as an infant and child will probably grow up and learn healthy habits and behaviors that will lead to secure attachments and relationships with others. By the same token, we often see that children who experience neglect, abuse or other types of trauma will struggle and tend to form anxious attachments or avoid them altogether. While some wounds may be a product of intended consequences, occasionally, some are a result of unintended consequences. For instance, even if you were beautifully cared for and nurtured a little too much as an infant, it might create major pain for you later in life if someone else *doesn't* replicate that kind of attention. After all, not everyone will have the skills or believe the world revolves around you. That will throw some people for a loop if they were coddled a little too much. It is a real challenge for the children of "helicopter parents" who hovered nearby so much the kids never learned to face adversity.

What if your experience was the opposite? What if you felt invisible, worthless, unloved and abandoned by caretakers who seemed indifferent to your needs for any reason whatsoever? Can you see how a child raised in those circumstances might set up a lifetime dynamic of feeling like they don't matter and then constantly recreating that dynamic, even if they attract a loving, caring partner?

Here's yet another possibility. What if you were raised in an amazingly indulgent environment where you were loved and adored, but for whatever reason, in your perspective as a child, you felt unloved or maybe even victimized? The truth is, oftentimes, our experiences are more shaped by our perspectives, impressions and "the stories we tell" rather than provable "facts" supported by evidence. I've had many clients, and even my own daughter, who felt that their parents' need to work made it appear that "they didn't care" despite the fact that they had many examples of loving behavior that revealed just the opposite. Sometimes even the most doting caretakers may cause some form of fear of neglect in young children. The "story" of one's childhood is almost entirely based on the perspective of the receiver, or the child, and for those of us who are adults with life experience and wisdom, we can probably anticipate some challenges with giving *that* kind of power to a child under seven years old. When you're 100% reliant on the kindness and care of others for your very survival, have very little life experience and no concept of patience or delayed gratification, it creates a bit of a distorted reality. In fact, it's in learning that your needs *will* be met that we learn to trust and form healthy bonds.

We don't let five-year-old children drive because they don't have the experience, wisdom, judgment or even motor skills to make that a good idea. But every adult walking around today, including you and me, dear reader, is highly influenced subconsciously by an idea they developed right around that time and carry around still. Children are, by nature, myopic because they (understandably) think the whole world revolves around them. While that may seem sweet and perhaps noble on one level, we'd all have to acknowledge it's just not practical or remotely true. With hundreds of millions of people now populating the world, it's pretty obvious the world can't revolve around us *all.*

Let me clarify a few things here. I'm not discounting children, their ability to speak their truth, or anyone's specific experience. I'm not victim blaming or excusing those who cause trauma to innocent children. Far from it, I assure you. I do what I do *because* I protect the innocent and I want to promote learning and healing for all. In order to understand the concept of C.O.R.E. wounds and R.O.O.T. issues, we need to acknowledge their connection to Relationship Origins of Trauma. When we finally get how and why we're attracting our current conditions, we can begin to address *what* we need to do to resolve the issues beneath those conditions and attract what we really desire.

A Quick Word about Trauma

At first glance, I'm sure the mere mention of a word like trauma in my acronym is anything but welcome, exciting or hopeful. However, it's an important distinction that I hope you'll take on and see as the path to what you ultimately want instead of something to fear or avoid. After all, it's a reference to *past* trauma you already experienced and now *get to heal.* It's not a threat of all-new trauma still to come, so there's nothing really here to fear. You've already made it through the worst of it and you're okay.

For those who resist acknowledging my description of a R.O.O.T. problem as Relationship Origin Of Trauma, I invite you to reconsider. Even if you think it's not a R.O.O.T. problem, I promise you, it is. Even if you think you never had trauma, I promise you, you did. Relationship trauma hides in your subconscious. Out of sight. Out of mind. It only gets triggered and comes into view under stress. It happens when there's a fight, or your feelings get hurt, or there's a breakup. Oh, and by the way, all those things are called trauma. And every time it happens, it stacks, and potentially gets much worse, unless you discover the R.O.O.T. and pull it right out.

When you finally understand that there is such a thing as your own personal Relationship Origin Of Trauma, it holds the key that unlocks the door to everything you always wanted. When you understand where it all began AND that it's simultaneously the root of everything that still challenges you, you can begin to realize the fact that you're almost full circle and close to resolving the very thing that invisibly frustrated you for so long.

Let's get a few things straight about this whole concept of understanding your own unique R.O.O.T. or Relationship Origin Of Trauma. For starters, we *all* have one, so it doesn't mean you're broken, messed up, unlovable or anything like that. If you're human, and you were raised by humans, *you* have a Relationship Origin Of Trauma. So, let's all just embrace it and stop denying it. There's no shame or guilt. In fact, shame and guilt are two of the biggest and most pervasive R.O.O.T.s that keep more people stuck than perhaps any other. So, let's just let them go and *choose healing* right now, in this moment. If you're ready to heal and drop the old BS or "belief system" that got you stuck in the first place, read on and let's continue.

Now is the time to understand that your R.O.O.T. cause is 100% specific to *you* and you alone. Just like mine is unique to me, yours is unique to you. However, while we all have our own version of a R.O.O.T., there's a *whole lot* of overlap between individuals as well. In fact, in a later chapter, I'll cover how on a planet of billions of individuals, all of our wounds tend to originate primarily in about twelve categories. At the end of the day, the one thing all of your relationship struggles or even failures have in common is *you*. Doesn't it seem a little unlikely that someone could continue to struggle with the same old relationship issues over and over again, even with brand new partners? If you want to call that a coincidence, or a series of them, that starts to defy reason. So, let's address you and your R.O.O.T., so you can be free.

R.O.O.T. Issues Lead to C.O.R.E. Wounds

As long as we're talking about the very same issues coming up again and again with different people, that hallmark is how we know we're dealing with a C.O.R.E. wound. I define a C.O.R.E. wound as one that is based on Continuous Or Recurring Experiences. Do you keep experiencing partners who cheat on you? That may be a C.O.R.E. wound. Have you been abused by multiple partners? That's probably a C.O.R.E. wound. Are substance abuse issues a recurring theme for you? That may be a C.O.R.E. wound, too. Again, the important distinction that can help break up this pattern for good is a recognition that it's not happening to torture you. It's only happening to teach you. It's really hard to identify something hugely relevant and important to you if it only happens one time. That could be an anomaly. However, when it becomes a pattern, and not just happenstance, it starts to get your attention.

Types of Wounds

There simply aren't that many different types of wounds and they all come down to sub-categories of the two universal fears.

31

The first universal fear is that in one way or another, we feel that *we're not enough.* Maybe it's not smart enough, attractive enough, gifted enough, kind enough, rich enough, successful enough…I could go on for days. The second universal fear is that you won't be loved. It could actually be considered as the root of the root when it comes to R.O.O.T.s because if you believe you're not enough in some way, the only logical and emotional conclusion is that you *won't be loved.*

When you understand that your specific R.O.O.T or Relationship Origin Of Trauma is the exact reason *you* struggle in relationships and that it will continue to sabotage you again and again until you put it to rest, I hope that will give you the leverage to step up and do the work to set yourself free. Just imagine what the world would look like and be like if everyone healed their own individual wounds all at one time. There would be no fears, no insecurities, no disputes, no injustice, no wars, no violence. Those things simply wouldn't be necessary. Now while that may sound a little naive and idealistic, the thing to remember is that you absolutely *can* finally heal it if you have the desire and courage to address it.

When Is a Good Time to Heal It?

It doesn't matter if you're in a relationship, out of one, praying for one or planning your escape. It doesn't matter who you date, who you marry or even how many times you marry. And if you say you don't want a relationship, *that* is the definition of a R.O.O.T. issue. No matter where you are, now would be a great time to continue reading so you can heal this for good. I've helped countless people who once struggled in relationships heal the wounds that kept them struggling which led them to find love and get married.

Your R.O.O.T. Issue Checklist

Use this quick checklist to identify some of the common signs and symptoms of ROOT issues:

R.O.O.T. issues for singles:

❑ Do you struggle in relationships?
❑ Do you feel jaded about the topic of love itself?
❑ Do you attract the same wrong partners again and again?
❑ Does it seem like no matter what, you just can't find love?
❑ Do you struggle to even find a date?!?
❑ Is relationship too painful to even think about?
❑ Have you already given up on love?
❑ Are you afraid you don't even deserve love?
❑ Do you put up walls with prospective partners?
❑ Do uncontrollable emotions sabotage you?
❑ Are you afraid people will leave you?

R.O.O.T. issues for couples:

❑ Do you feel tender or sometimes walk on eggshells with your partner?
❑ Do you get more and more guarded or put up walls with others?
❑ Do you find yourself getting or staying angry at one another?
❑ Have you lost confidence or radiance, or have you never had it in your relationship?
❑ Do you feel like you lost your faith in people, or in your love?
❑ Are you starting to think you'll never have love even though you are in a relationship?
❑ Or worse yet...are you afraid you don't even deserve love?

If you answered yes to any of those things, I *promise* you that a R.O.O.T. issue is sabotaging you right now in real time. And I also promise you, this book holds the answer you seek so keep reading.

Chapter 3:

Here We Go Again… or Why the Hell Does this Keep Happening⁈

As I start from the very beginning and walk you through to the happy ending on the other side where you are finally prepared to manifest your mate from a place of healing and peace, I want to make sure you know exactly *how* and *why* you got here in the first place. It's a critical distinction because those who lack awareness or fail to learn the lessons they needed will surely end up right back where they started until they finally get what they needed to learn. For example, there's a reason you're not expected to show up for your third-grade class this week. That's because you have, I presume, satisfied the requirements of your school district by mastering all the skills and knowledge that a third grader where you live is expected to master. Although the lessons are far more complex at your age and stage, compared to the average third grader, and they

35

are much more personal in nature, they are no less critical to your success long term.

The lessons we're here to learn, master and ultimately heal have to do with your capacity to establish, nurture and maintain human relationships with others. Although I don't often make assumptions without further investigating, I'm going to operate under the premise that there is a specific and solid reason why you would pick up a book called *"Same Sh*t. Different Date: Why You Keep Attracting the Same Wrong Partners – and How to Finally Solve It!"* I suspect at some level, you have a realization that there is value for you within these pages, otherwise you would never invest the time or energy to read it.

It is here where I will drop my assumptions about what you may or may not already know or realize. As I've already pointed out in the previous chapter, the one thing you have in common with all your past "dating disasters" is you. Maybe someone simply recommended that you read this book. Perhaps you only have the barest of inklings that you may be somehow contributing to a pattern of similar "types" that you may be attracting. Still others might know exactly what kind of hot mess they get drawn to every single time; they just might not have any earthly idea how to fix it. The good news is that I'm writing this book for all of you and I intend to give you everything you will possibly need to identify where you are now, what you need to learn, or how you can get to the place where high-quality, exceptional partners are attracted to and pursue *you*. So, let's get started.

Relationships and Wounds

Relationships and wounds will always go together and you will never in this lifetime have one without the other. Aren't you glad you picked up this happy, little book? Now before you get discouraged and throw the book out the window, the main reason there is a linkage between the wounds that cause pain and the relationships that bring pleasure is that most people take the wounds of relationship personally at some level. They think it's somehow their fault or it's related to their personal worth. The problem with that is that over time, stacked pain in the form of failed relationships tends to make one feel like they're somehow broken, star-crossed or just defective. They may even start to panic when they think they'll never have love or that it's just not in the future for them. I promise you: *that* is not true.

The reason we have, and will always have, pain and pleasure linked to our relationships is because it's simply in the natural order of the universe to maintain balance at all times. It's not and never has been "personal." There's no way to have day without night any more than you can have black without white, up without down or hot without cold. In Asian cultures, the concept of yin and yang are a visual representation of a continuously linked and dynamic flow of perfect balance in harmony with its equal and opposite energy. You can't choose to never get sick and only have exceptional health in unending perpetuity. It doesn't work that way. In fact, oftentimes what you experience as "sick" is simply your body's attempt to restore balance to the system. Fevers, sneezing, runny noses: what you experience as an absence of health is actually your immune system's way of burning off or

37

expelling that which is causing the problem so you can return to balance and good health. In essence, with a slight shift in perspective, what you may see as the "sickness" is also simultaneously the "cure."

In much the same way, wounds and relationships, or more specifically, pain and pleasure, are also a form of yin and yang that are inseparable and completely necessary. Although I've only mentioned two-part dualities to explain the concept, relationships actually offer three possibilities when it comes to results. Here's the reality that you need to know: relationships have three possible outcomes and sometimes they are simultaneous or even interchangeable.

1) Relationships Wound Us

From the moment we are born, and until the day we die, relationships have the potential to wound us. When our needs are met with love and care, we bond, connect and feel safe. However, when we don't receive what we want or need quickly, our brains begin to link up disempowering meanings. If people hurt us, disappoint us, ignore us or even abuse us, it creates wounds that we carry around in the form of fears, insecurities, even terrifying phobic responses in the most dramatic cases.

2) Relationships Trigger Us

The intermediate step in this system, and it *is* a system, is that we also get triggered in our relationships. For instance, if someone ignores you, calls you a name or even abuses you and it reminds you of a prior time when you weren't seen, heard or appreciated the way you hoped, it could very well trigger an emotional response. Whether the response is anger, fear, sadness or even violence, it's always directly related to one's perception of the severity of the original wound. Now that word "perception" is an important distinction because what causes terror for one may be overlooked entirely by another with different experiences, values, beliefs or ideals. We're going to talk a lot more about that in the pages ahead.

3) Relationships Heal Us

That's right. It's always at least a three-part process. What causes all the pain, frustration and intense suffering is that most people bounce back and forth between first stage wounds and second stage triggers. It's almost like they never even realize that healing is what's possible and ultimately called for in order to transcend, or should I say, *trance end,* the perception of pain. Again, we'll be talking *a lot* more about this healing process in the pages ahead. After all, that's why you bought this book and if you truly want to be healed for good, and you make it a MUST, I am absolutely committed to making that happen for you.

Chapter 4:

Soul Mate or Soul Messenger? They Both Come to Serve

 As a relationship coach who works with clients all over the globe, I get a rare perspective on watching my client's response when they meet a new prospective partner that seemingly "ticks all the boxes." There have been many who have turned out to be the "real deal" that led to marriage, partially because I help my clients get to the place where they finally discover and heal the unresolved wounds they had. Of course, I've also seen my share of hot and heavy romances that fizzled out rather quickly after a promising start. As a result, I've given a great deal of thought to that magical and elusive formula that makes the difference between a love that's built to last and one that's soon in the past. You may be surprised to know that when someone starts throwing around the word "soul mate" or even worse, a term I particularly dislike "twin flames," a little too prematurely, I consider that a red flag in some ways.

Frankly, I think those descriptors are both over-used and even more misunderstood.

So, You Met Your "Soul Mate," Huh?

The term soul mate has so many meanings that have entered the pop culture lexicon and get attached to these words. Words like "perfect" start getting thrown around indiscriminately. Amazing. Too good to be true. A Godsend. Whew, boy. When I hear words like this from my clients regarding someone they just met, I have to confess, I get more suspicious than elated. It's not that I'm jaded or negative on the concept of true love. Far from it. It's just that I've seen it and heard it so many times that I know those words are usually more indicative of some kind of fantasy skewed through rose-colored glasses than a realistic and grounded appraisal of a new prospective partner. Let's be clear: if it's going to be a sustainable love for the ages, it's not going to endure if it's based on a cocktail of dopamine and hormones. That's called infatuation and it is not built to last.

Get Them Off the Pedestal

In my line of work, it's fairly obvious that I particularly appreciate the idea and notion of love as much as anyone. However, I'm partial to the kind of love that's not based on a fantasy of a perfect partner perched upon a pedestal (that's a lot of alliteration, isn't it?). Likewise, I'm no fan of putting people in the "pit" either and attributing only negative characteristics to them. The problem with putting people either on a pedestal or in the pit is that it artificially creates distance between them and you. That's not a healthy, balanced and loving relationship if you idolize someone and elevate them literally *above* you which automatically can *only* mean that in comparison, you are beneath them figuratively and possibly even literally. At the same time, when you put someone in the pit by demonizing them and focusing only on their non-redeeming traits, you will never be able to have a satisfactory relationship of any kind with them due to your one-sided impression of them. The point is, you can't possibly have a quality relationship of equals if you metaphorically "look down upon" someone or objectify them by "looking up to them" and feeling inferior. That's far from healthy or helpful and I don't recommend it at all.

This whole concept of the pedestal and the pit is something I learned from one of my very wise mentors, Dr. John DeMartini. He is known for saying, and I'm paraphrasing here, "When you take people off the pedestal or out of the pit, you can put them in your heart where they belong." In fact, I mention his name here to demonstrate a key point. I honor John with attribution and compliments out of a healthy sense of respect and appreciation for a man whose intellect and genius I truly admire. Yet, at the same time, I have no need or desire to subjugate myself or subordinate my own contribution. I'm actually comfortable acknowledging myself right alongside him because he's the one who taught me to seek out the "traits of the greats" and identify them in myself as well. As they say, "if you spot it, you got it" and I'm proud that I have many of the same traits that I admire so much in my friend, John. What do you think might happen if you emulated that same kind of respect for others with respect for self? If it sounds like something you admire or would like to emulate, I invite you to incorporate it into your relationships. At the same time, I want to acknowledge you because you've *already* gotten one of this book's principle messages and we're just getting started. You deserve to embrace your own greatness, and if you can do that with humility also, that is a level of mastery that is truly extraordinary. Well done.

There's also one other common denominator that seems to precede words like "soul mate" or "twin flame." Often those impressions are the product of a very limited sampling. In other words, their time with this new potential partner has been incredibly short. One date. Two dates. A magical weekend. Maybe even a few weeks. It's still based on an impression that's somewhat limited in terms of its length and depth. After all, you have to expect that whenever you first meet a new potential partner, people tend to be on their best behavior. It's almost like each person's public relations agent shows up as their personal representative in those heady early days, especially if there is an attraction. In fact, there's almost a literal, direct correlation between how much someone is attracted to a person and the effort to which they will go to be on their best behavior.

In addition, let me add one other important side note. Again, my work with people all over the globe gives me access to more highly personal dating experiences than most any individual will have no matter how often they date. That's because I'm getting reports from the front lines of their individual dating experience nearly every single day when I'm coaching them. Believe me, that adds up to a lot of insight across multiple individuals, countries, cultures, customs, you name it. When my client gets too high on a brand-new date, I will often tend to step in as a moderating voice. It's not that I'm trying to rain on their parade. Far from it. It's just that I don't want *my* clients losing themselves in the fantasy and letting it affect their good judgment, hard work and how they show up on their dates. While that's more than enough of a reason right there for offering a valuable perspective check, in all honesty, there's an even more sinister scenario that drives my response. Too often, that whole "sweep them off their feet and convince them that their whole lives have led to this very moment when they finally met" is a page right out of the playbook of a narcissist or a sociopath. I mention this specifically because individuals with personality disorders have a unique gift for detecting the *exact* types of unresolved wounds that allow them to run roughshod over that person while creating a great deal of pain and suffering for their intended target.

Let me just say this: if this book helps you avoid a relationship with a narcissist, and that is one goal here, it will be worth far more than any price you could have possibly paid.

So, What Exactly Is a Soul Mate?

Merriam Webster defines the term soul mate as 1: a person who is perfectly suited to another in temperament or 2: a person who strongly resembles another in attitudes or beliefs. While those are the dictionary meanings of the term, those definitions are a little limited in their dimension. For my purpose, I believe Elizabeth Gilbert touched on an outstanding point in her runaway best-selling book, *Eat Pray Love.* Here's how she defines a soul mate, the one that hasn't inspired a thousand poets and dreamers:

"People think a soul mate is your perfect fit, and that's what everyone wants. But a true soul mate is a mirror, the person who shows you everything that is holding you back, the person who brings you to your own attention so you can change your life.

A true soul mate is probably the most important person you'll ever meet, because they tear down your walls and smack you awake. But to live with a soul mate forever? Nah. Too painful. Soul mates, they come into your life just to reveal another layer of yourself to you, and then leave.

A soul mate's purpose is to shake you up, tear apart your ego a little bit, show you your obstacles and addictions, break your heart open so new light can get in, make you so desperate and out of control that you have to transform your life, then introduce you to your spiritual master..."

While I agree with her on the critical nature of that job in our collective emotional, cognitive and spiritual development, I submit that perhaps a more descriptive name might make this distinction more clear and easier to understand. I propose the adoption of a second term that is far more accurate: I call this person who shows up in your life to serve you by bringing to light critical life lessons your *Soul Messenger*. I like this term because it prepares you for their entrance, welcomes the contribution as positive and presupposes its value to your soul's journey. Perhaps, just as important, I like what it doesn't promote or promise. The term Soul Messenger values the role without the sting of a promise unfulfilled in the event it doesn't turn out to be your one and only lifetime partner. However, it *still* holds open the possibility that it just might *be* a love for the ages. It seems to me that the question of Soul Mate or Soul Messenger just might be best answered *over time* with a clear-eyed mix of emotion *and* reason.

Think about it: so much of the shame and guilt that is part and parcel of a breakup or divorce lies in the concept or appearance of failure on the part of one or both parties. It is this expectation of some type of forever-and-always fantasy where a couple magically lives "happily ever after" that is at the root of a great deal of the disfunction that keeps people stuck and struggling. What if we welcomed loving experiences that taught us a lesson or brought us needed gifts and celebrated them with gratitude instead of retreating into scarcity-based fears of not being enough? That's the area that keeps more people suffering than any other because of their presumption or perception of failure. It's like people who invest time or effort in relationships have some sort of belief that they always have to win at any cost, even if they themselves know at some level that there are some serious flaws in the union. Even if you ask people prior to being "in" a relationship, nearly all of them would admit they fully realize that not all dates turn into mates. Then, something happens once they're dating, and it becomes 'unite at all costs'...but why?

It's our ego that engages and resists the feeling of "rejection" because it's just too painful to ponder that for whatever reason, we are perceived as "not enough" in some way. Many people, in an attempt to maintain certainty and the status quo, may tend to stay in a relationship where they have serious doubts and concerns rather than rock the boat by gambling on whether they could attract another partner who's equal or even better than their current partner.

Love by the Numbers

In order to drive home a critical point in my thinking behind the whole Soul Mate versus Soul Messenger designation, let's look at it in the form of a rough mathematical equation because numbers don't lie. I asked one of my groups recently how many people the average person will date, even once, in the course of a lifetime. Now, there are outliers in every generalization like the high school sweethearts who marry, never having dated another person, and the serial daters and commitment-phobic individuals who are artificially inflating the other extreme with maybe hundreds of dates. So, while making the point, the group consensus was that people might date between 30 to 50 people over a lifetime. So, let's split the difference and called it 40.

Then, I asked how many long-term relationships would you say is the average and I defined long-term as a relationship that lasts at least a year or more or might even turn into a live-in or spouse. The consensus was maybe four of them might meet that criteria. So, if that was the breakdown, that means four long-term relationships (and to be clear, I'm not conflating that with a soul mate) might develop over the course of maybe 40 different partners. That adds up to a one-in-ten ratio of "success," and by some definitions, a 90% *failure rate.* (Of course, your actual numbers may vary.) That means that by design, most dates *aren't ever supposed to be great matches.* That's literally what the numbers reflect. Yet, still, people's ego or essential need for certainty gets them hung up on the need to "make things work" even when they know it's not working, and it probably can't work long-term.

I can tell you that every time I work with a client who's wounded by the appearance of "rejection" or frustration with dating, they either point to a couple of experiences they wanted to work out that didn't for whatever reason, or they point to ones that didn't go anywhere, even if they aren't bothered by the fact that those specific relationships didn't go anywhere. In other words, some people will *simultaneously* use the fact that 90% of their dates didn't work out, while others will point to the handful of relationships (the maybe 10% we estimated previously) that went well enough for a period of time but ultimately ended for one reason or another in order to come to the same rotten conclusion: that there's something wrong with them. Then they use that to doubt their worth and reinforce the fact that they are somehow "unlovable." It's like they only use the sampling that supports their terrible narrative or story of woe and validates their sadness. Is it me or does that also strike you as unfair? How does *anyone* win when you use both your successes and perceived failures as a reason to beat yourself up unfairly?

I've even had clients who use their sad stories again and again because they're addicted to them. For instance, just last week, I had a client who was shocked to realize that he was addicted to pity because it was far easier to experience connection through sharing his sad story over and over again and staying stuck than to solve his problem, be a leader and step out of learned helplessness. Ironically, he wasn't even aware that he was doing it. He just knew it worked because he was used to getting rewarded for his brokenness. Time and again, his girlfriend would try to support him and give him pep talks until she finally hit her breaking point and couldn't take it anymore. I pointed out how there was no way a woman he wanted to marry and take care of forever could ever trust a man she pitied. When I finally bottom-lined it for him that way, he was filled with regret and saw quickly how he had totally sabotaged what he considered his best relationship ever. However, by then, it was too late. The damage was done, all because he focused on the sad part of his story that validated his inability to overcome the very real disfunction from his past. Now that he had this realization, we can begin to work through his past in order to release the story and create a far more compelling future. Although it was a hard lesson to learn, once he saw it, it was ultimately one that will change him "for good." Chalk it up to another lesson courtesy of a Soul Messenger.

Skewed Data, Skewed Results

Let's change the context on my previous point illustrated using numbers. How can you get a consistent, realistic or reliable appraisal of *anything* if you cherry-pick the numbers and only use a portion of the "raw data" that supports your already pre-conceived and terrible conclusion? You would never do that with actual research, voting or polling numbers. You can't say a particular prescription drug is 100% effective for patients who need it by just deleting the 4 people who died from complications the drug caused. You can't say 100% of taxpayers support a rezoning issue by just ignoring the staggering number of people who voted against it or didn't vote at all. Likewise, any time you see a leader re-elected with 90+% of the vote, you know it's propaganda and not a legitimate result. That's because 90% of humans will most likely never agree on anything unless the sampling is so targeted as to eliminate variables. In other words, when you see a result that one-sided, someone is cooking the books. The point is, people do this every day by choosing what they focus on and that *choice* has very real and far-reaching consequences, even if you're not aware of it when you make the choice.

The Bottom Line

Whether your partner turns out to be a Soul Mate or a Soul Messenger, my recommendation is to be wide open to the possibilities and learnings that they came to offer. Welcome them with arms and heart wide open and get the lessons they offer through a filter of love, compassion and understanding for them and especially for you. After all, no matter how it all goes, they *still* came to heal you ultimately. If you really *knew* that in your heart and soul, for sure, in advance, it just might change the way you show up in your relationships. If that's the case, this book has, again, changed your life – and that's why I wrote it.

Chapter 5:

Magical Morphing Messengers

 In the previous chapters, I mentioned in passing that when we don't get the lesson the first time, or the second, or the third time, it just means you will be guaranteed to be presented with the lesson again. Such a bold statement begs a simple question: how can people continue to be presented with the same lesson again and again? In other words, don't they ever learn from past mistakes and stop making the same poor choices over and over?

Well, It's Not That Simple

Yes, while there are some people who seldom learn their lessons, most people get the message and change their behavior accordingly. Pain has a way of being an outstanding teacher. However, this oversimplification of a complex situation ignores a key concept you need to know so you can prepare and prevent it from happening to you.

That concept is called the Magical Morphing Messenger. As I said in the previous chapter, people who come into your life for a reason or a season probably don't really qualify as soul mates, despite the fact that the lessons they come to deliver are powerful, profound and life changing. That's why I coined the term Soul Messenger because I think it helps to put their role in context. Even if they don't stay long, their role is still vitally important. Plus, when we understand and expect messengers will come into our lives to simply deliver a message and move on, it takes some of the sting out of a connection that was never meant to last a lifetime anyway. After all, no one expects a messenger to hang around once their message is delivered. Once we get the message, we sign for it, smile and wish them well on their way as they deliver their next message to a recipient who also needs what they've come to deliver. The lasting pain occurs when we tell ourselves the story of the one that shouldn't have gotten away.

Here's Where It Gets Tricky

For those who may be slow to get the lesson, or overlook it entirely, even multiple times, that should not be an indictment of their intelligence or their awareness. In fact, that's kind of an unfair expectation. The reason most people miss the message is due to what I call the Magical Morphing Messenger. The problem is that this type of messenger doesn't show up in a colorful uniform with a logo on their shirt. This kind of messenger shows up incognito and is cleverly concealed in a brand-new disguise each and every time one approaches. That makes it very difficult to identify a messenger in disguise. Plus, it's even more difficult to identify them before they identify *themselves.* Sometimes we never even realize they dropped their message and left. Most of the time, a messenger is on their very best professional behavior because no one opens the door and invites in the stranger who seems suspect or even dangerous. Most people can't even identify the messenger until they pass through and deliver the message. This may be slightly confusing so let me give you a real-life example of the Magical Morphing Messenger in action.

Melinda's Story

It's too hard to get how this works in a theoretical, third-party description so with her permission, I am using a client's story because it is an outstanding example of how the Magical Morphing Messenger can operate so stealthily, especially when you're not aware of the concept and have never even heard the term.

It all started, as it usually does, when Melinda was a child. She learned at a very young age that her mother was not to be challenged. She was a very strong force who ruled by intimidation and a "my way or the highway" kind of certainty. Most of the time, Melinda was pretty restrained and didn't challenge her Mom's authority. But in her teen years, a time when kids are *expected* to rebel a little and begin to think for themselves and question authority in preparation for adulthood, there was one incident that got pretty heated. In fact, it got so heated that she ended up getting kicked out of her mother's house. I don't mean just kicked out like go away and cool off while you learn your lesson. I mean call the police and leave her with "nowhere to go" kind of kicked out. So, she actually ended up being held in a mental institution until her father could return from a business trip to pick her up and take her to another state to live. Imagine the trauma of being uprooted from your life with no guarantees, no warning and being sent far away. She was banished to live in exile, no chance to say goodbye. She felt total shame and absolute fear about what happened.

As a result, she learned at a pretty young age that speaking up or voicing her truth equaled immediate, painful and extremely frightening rejection *and* abandonment. If that wasn't traumatic enough, as a result, she learned to copy-and-paste that terrible and inaccurate belief over every single scenario that felt even remotely similar. She learned that love could equal massive pain and punishment, and no one really gives a damn what she thinks, feels or needs. She learned to zip it or face immediate excommunication from the family unit. Talk about a huge wound and severe consequences for such a young teen who had no concept of adult responsibilities and survival. This set-in motion a series of events, or should I say messengers, that still continues today, nearly three decades later.

One of the first messengers who came to teach Melinda was a first love that she dated for a few years. There was some talk of marriage but along the way, some disagreements escalated and they decided to go their separate ways. Some time later, she heard that this man had gotten a serious, life-threatening medical diagnosis, so he decided to move back to his country where he had family who may be able to help care for him. Not long after, she heard that the man passed away on the other side of the world. As is often the case, we humans tend to long for what we feel we can't have. So, her connection to him deepened as she questioned this painful series of events and wondered "what if" over and over again. She couldn't be with him when he needed her most and you'll never guess what familiar lesson she took from it. She gleaned that if she had just kept her mouth shut, they might have stayed together and she wouldn't have been rejected and abandoned. Sound familiar? It was a copy-and-paste of the wound her mom had created years earlier. Now, of course, one could make the case that the message she took away lost a great deal in the translation, but that's not how this works. Messenger number one's message had now been delivered and his assignment was complete.

Some time later, after nursing that fresh wound created by the death of a man she loved and cared for, she began to live again and found a new boyfriend. This seemed like a positive step in the right direction and a sign that some healing had taken place since she was being vulnerable and open to love once again. In fact, things started to go pretty well and one day, she found herself accepting this new man's wedding proposal. Things were really looking up and she began to get comfortable with her new life and plan a wedding that truly made her happy. Unfortunately, since planning a wedding can be a stressful experience, as the big day got closer, the couple began to find themselves further apart. Then, with one final disagreement in plans, seven weeks from their wedding date, with invitations sent, her partner announced that he no longer wanted to marry her and she needed to move out of the only house she knew, immediately. Sound familiar? I'll bet you'll never guess what message she got from what was now messenger number two. She learned that if she had just kept her mouth shut, they might have stayed together, and she wouldn't have been rejected and abandoned. Oh, and if that wasn't enough, she now had to deal with the shame and guilt that came from having to explain what happened to pretty much everyone she knew. I'm sure you can imagine the pain at this point; but that's still not where this story ends.

As you might imagine, there were many years where Melinda equated relationships with massive pain and avoided them altogether. In fact, she probably sabotaged a bunch of them before they even went anywhere at all because that's what you do when your only reference for love is massive pain. So, she threw herself into her work and built a very nice business where she can safely express her care and love to her clients from a much safer, and less risky, distance. In fact, her primary focus in life became this growing business where she could share her gifts and help people because it felt good. At one point it began to grow and as a way to fuel her growth, she took on a new office space that was pretty great but just a little beyond her comfort zone financially. Being a smart businesswoman, she sought a way to make it happen by bringing on a friend who was a complementary practitioner who could lease out one of her offices. That way it turned out to be a win/win since she could help a friend, get a better office space and save money all at the same time. It was working perfectly right up to where, you guessed it, her renter decided she could no longer afford the space so she wanted out of the lease that was co-signed, backed financially and perfectly legal. Or so she thought.

One thing led to another and the partnership unraveled as attorneys were retained. I'll bet you'll never guess what thought silently popped up in the back of her mind as the lawyers sorted out the details and she struggled with feeling like a failure once again. By now, you're starting to see how this works. That's right. That old voice in the back of her head from three decades of experience was sounding off even when it wasn't related to a loving or intimate relationship. It was spilling over into a business relationship! Now her wound was starting to morph also. It was no longer about just keeping her mouth shut so she wouldn't be rejected and abandoned. It was about why do people always let me down and I end up alone, once again, every time. Why do I *always* have to work so hard to compensate for other people who never do what they say or honor the commitments they make? Can you see how this is magically morphing over time and metastasizing into an absolute cancer on more and more of her relationships and connections with others? The problem is that every single time it happens, she pulls in and disconnects from others even more. She trusts less. She's open and vulnerable less. She accepts less and puts more stress on herself to over-compensate.

As I said, this time she wasn't even aware of how this pattern had just jumped from her personal life to her professional life because it was so hidden in her subconscious and in a totally different sphere of her life. However, since she had been speaking with me and I knew her pattern, I was able to point out that this was definitely a case of what I call "same sh*t. different date." This issue was going to keep happening *for her* so that she could ultimately *heal it.*

With this new awareness of what, why and how it's happening, we will create a new meaning and heal it for good. How, you ask? Keep reading and I'll show you how to identify and heal your old wounds that no longer serve you. For good.

Chapter 6:

"My Ex Did a Number on Me."
How to Identify Recurring Patterns

 Most people are completely unaware of the fact that they still have lingering wounds from childhood. They have no idea that they don't just disappear out of sight, out of mind. They certainly aren't aware that they are still silently, secretly affected by them. Plus, they have no clue that familiar lessons come to serve them, not torture them. Now that you are aware of these facts, I want to help you dig in and identify any possible lingering issues so they can be healed.

While this new awareness you now have is the critical first step, it can still be challenging to identify painful issues from the past. For starters, we naively assume that challenges that popped up with one past partner will never, ever happen again after you break up with that person. That's probably not true. Furthermore, we seldom look for recurring issues between partners unless it's in a reactive way. For example, after a particularly "familiar" disappointment, one might create a new resolve to never do "x" again. That's on the right track but it misses the point. I suggest we take a look at those old issues in a *proactive* way instead of a reactive way.

There's another reason old challenges live on out of sight and out of mind. Humans can be remarkably resilient so we have a tendency to "paper over" or cover up old issues from the past. We may try to rationalize them or explain them away or even forget them altogether but that doesn't solve anything. It's like renovating a very old house and putting new wallpaper over damaged and peeling walls marred by bumps and imperfections. That's never going to work well or look good unless you take the time to do the work properly.

Let's get started with a quick priming exercise that will help you scan for some relevant issues that deserve your attention in the coming chapters and exercises. We're going to do a quick, collective post-mortem on all your most significant relationships in order to look for patterns you may want to bring to your awareness so we can work on them and put them to rest. For good.

Step One

Before we get to the part of this exercise where we look at past partners, we want to start at the very beginning and keep it simple. In this case, the beginning is your childhood. I'm going to provide you with a list of situations, issues and wounds that may or may not have happened to you in your younger years. Keep in mind, we want to place a particular emphasis on your earlier years through age seven because those are the foundational years. However, whether it happened at three, 12 or 17 years old, I want you to take note of it either in your own notebook or journal or in the workbook I specifically designed and created for buyers of this book. That workbook is available separately via Amazon and is appropriately called *Companion. Peace.* and that's not just a clever title. It's what I truly wish for you as a result of doing this work. I think you'll also benefit by doing all of this work together in one neat, organized journal that prompts you with specific assignments and plenty of space to write your answers and keep important notes.

In any event, however you decide to record your answers, let's just account for any events or experiences that happened at any age and write them down. We can figure out later whether it's relevant or not.

Connecting the Dots

Like any good 'connect-the-dots' exercise, we will use the numbers provided next to each possible answer and connect them in order to reveal the bigger picture. However, you won't actually be drawing lines on a page to reveal that hidden picture. In this exercise, the numbers you connect, themselves, will give you a very clear picture of everything you need to see. I've set it up this way to simplify it for you when it comes to immediately seeing patterns, so be sure to circle the number next to any word you did experience or, if you are keeping track in a separate book, write down the number. For instance, the first answer in the list below just happens to be the word "divorce." So, the question you will ask yourself is:

• **As a child, did I experience a <u>divorce?</u>**

Identifying Recurring Patterns

Circle THE NUMBER of any experience below that applies to you:

(1) Divorce
(2) Separation
(3) Death
(4) Incarceration
(5) Drug rehab
(6) Infidelity
(7) Family / Custody disputes
(8) Adoption
(9) Isolation
(10) Rejection
(11) Long distance romance
(12) Military service
(13) Job transfer
(14) Ghosted
(15) Sustained infrequent contact
(16) Non-payment of support
(17) Domestic violence

(18) Cyberbullying
(19) Humiliation
(20) Objectification
(21) Name calling
(22) Criticism / attacks
(23) Verbal threats
(24) Intimidation
(25) Manipulation
(26) Injustice
(27) Shame
(28) Betrayal
(29) Exploitation
(30) Massive uncertainty
(31) Distant / disinterested
(32) Gossiping
(33) Spreading lies or innuendo
(34) Substance abuse
(35) Sexual assault
(36) Mental illness

(37) Assault & battery
(38) Addictions
(39) Neglect
(40) Emotional abuse
(41) Narcissism
(42) Personality disorders
(43) Rage / anger issues
(44) Communication issues
(45) Promiscuity cheating
(46) Eviction
(47) Adoption
(48) Foster care
(49) Step-parents
(50) Accidents
(51) Fire
(52) Floods
(53) Natural disasters
(54) War / terror

Obviously, I'm not talking about your divorce if you were only a child. I'm asking if your parents or primary caretakers experienced a divorce that affected *you*. If it did, you would circle the corresponding number 1 that goes with that answer. If it does not apply to you, simply skip that and move through the rest of the list circling or writing down the numbers you experienced.

Write any numbers that apply here:

_____

_____

_____

_____

Here's How This Works:

In step one, you identified past experiences that may have occurred in your childhood and we simply want to **identify it by the number at this stage.** This is done by design and it will all soon become clear. However, at this point, let's say you end up with a list of numbers that looks like this:

Number of Relevant Experiences from Childhood:

1, 3, 4, 7, 11, 13, 22, 23, 24, 29, 33, 37, 42

Since this phase refers to your own childhood experience, we will label it as **SCENARIO 1** and then move on to the next step.

Step Two

Next, we're going to skip ahead and start to scan our prior relationships giving particular emphasis to marriages, engagements, or live-in partners. We want to prioritize for those significant partners who were closest to you or lived with you or in close proximity. Then, let's identify any past partners based on duration of time together or emotional closeness. Let's also be sure to identify by name and include any partners who represented a significant emotional investment or even a painful breakup. The rule of thumb here is that the stronger the emotion you attach to the person, the stronger the clue. So do some digging. This is where we start to mine for the clues that will help you change everything. Here's an example of the format I want you to use:

Partner name: _____

Scenario #: _____

Significant memories/clues: _____

_____

_____

Relevant Number List: _____

_____

_____

_____

_____

As you list the partner names, feel free to jot down any reminders of significant issues that may feel relevant as you consider what wounds or issues might have come up while you were together. Maybe under your ex, you'd list a few key words like "spouse, divorced, cheating." Perhaps one might list "high school sweetheart, broke up for college." Next, be sure to accurately list all relevant numbers from the list you developed in Step One on the lines below. (If you use the *Companion. Peace.* workbook, you will be able to simply circle the corresponding numbers rather than rewrite them.) This is important because you will see clues, patterns and trends emerge numerically, visually.

Then, we'll do the exact same process for your next most important partner from the past. You may find that the numbers are nearly identical despite the fact that you're assessing two totally different people, different relationships and even different time periods perhaps decades apart. Or you may discover that the numbers look very different with little to no overlap. If that's the case, that's fine. We're simply looking for emerging patterns here.

Here's How Step 2 Works

Here's a quick example of what this step will look like as you complete it. I've shown 2 former partners below which we label as *scenarios* to keep the experiences separate but compare them at the same time. Since each individual partnership is a unique and individual story, we go back to the original list of 54 items and choose only the experiences that are relevant to that individual partner. Here are two examples below. Feel free to do as many former relationships as you can remember or that you find useful or pertinent. Trust your intuition to know who should be included and who doesn't need to be counted. Just remember, the stronger the emotion, the more important and relevant so use this opportunity to search for clues so we can connect the dots. Once you finish selecting and assessing your exes, let's move on to deciphering the patterns.

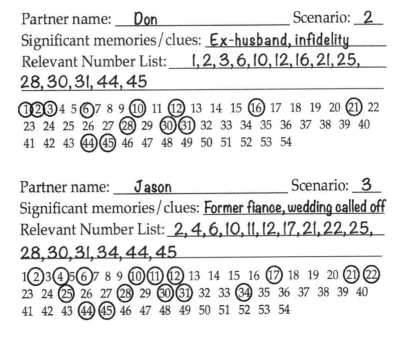

Partner name: __Don_____ Scenario: _2_
Significant memories/clues: __Ex-husband, infidelity__
Relevant Number List: __1, 2, 3, 6, 10, 12, 16, 21, 25,__
__28, 30, 31, 44, 45__
①②③ 4 5 ⑥ 7 8 9 ⑩ 11 ⑫ 13 14 15 ⑯ 17 18 19 20 ㉑ 22
23 24 25 26 27 ㉘ 29 ㉚ ㉛ 32 33 34 35 36 37 38 39 40
41 42 43 ㊹ ㊺ 46 47 48 49 50 51 52 53 54

Partner name: __Jason_____ Scenario: _3_
Significant memories/clues: __Former fiance, wedding called off__
Relevant Number List: __2, 4, 6, 10, 11, 12, 17, 21, 22, 25,__
__28, 30, 31, 34, 44, 45__
1 ② 3 ④ ⑤ ⑥ 7 8 9 ⑩ ⑪ ⑫ 13 14 15 16 ⑰ 18 19 20 ㉑ ㉒
23 24 ㉕ 26 27 ㉘ 29 ㉚ ㉛ 32 33 ㉞ 35 36 37 38 39 40
41 42 43 ㊹ ㊺ 46 47 48 49 50 51 52 53 54

Once you have completed the assignment for each former partner you've identified, first, let's note how many scenarios we reviewed to get that number. Remember, that would include both your own childhood which was scenario # 1 and then an additional scenario for each former significant other you evaluated. So, if you assessed your own childhood + 6 individual partners, your baseline number (or the denominator if presented as part of a fraction) would be the number 7. We'll need this number on the assessment so be sure you identify it.

Childhood scenario # 1 + 6 former partner scenarios = 7

Next, let's go back and circle or count all common numbers and track how many times each number gets circled.

Understanding Recurring Numbers

If you start to notice the same numbers popping up again and again as you rate individual former partners, you have just discovered a recurring issue that is trending across multiple partnerships. If that's the case, the assessment is working perfectly to illustrate patterns that may or may not have been consciously noticed. At the same time, you can expect to see numbers that are just as unique as your past partners. That's perfect and to be expected, too. For our purposes, we won't be focusing on those outliers.

For starters, let's identify the most common numbers and count how many times they show up individually. Any time a specific number pops up again and again on multiple partnerships, that qualifies as a pattern that simply cannot be ignored. You'll want to definitely note all of those by finding the highest numbers but, of course, count the smaller numbers as well. Let's say you see some high numbers like these:

10 = 7/7

22 = 7/7

31 = 5/7

44 = 3/7

Any time a number shows up across the board or in this case, 7 out of 7 scenarios, that is a red flag that you should definitely note and work on later in the book. Next, you identify those high-frequency issues from the key and you discover that #10 represents rejection and #22 represents criticism/attacks.

To continue with the example, if # 31 (which is Distant/disinterested) showed up in 5 out of 7 scenarios, that is also worth noting as statistically significant and I'd keep it on your radar to see how it shows up as part of your overall pattern. After all, it's almost predictable and hardly surprising that a partner's disinterest will frequently precede recurring feelings of rejection and criticism/attacks. Emotions and behaviors like that tend to show up together as a cause and effect. Likewise, if a number like 44 (Communication issues) showed up in 3 out of 7 scenarios, it's notable but not nearly as important as the high-scoring issues that show up again and again. It's a great example of where 20% of your focus will yield 80% of your results so focus on the big picture and don't get overwhelmed and bogged down in the details.

Identifying Categories

Once you've gone through and identified the numbers for all your past partners, it's time to look for the over-arching themes that may be recurring again and again. For your convenience and ease of use, this simple diagnostic tool will help you identify at a glance what you need to know. I clustered the issues and numbered them based on some of the most common unresolved wounds. In this case, they all fit into a simple A thru E answer key that breaks down as follows:

Answers 1 - 16 are related to possible **Abandonment Issues**
Answers 17 - 24 are related to possible **Bullying Issues**
Answers 25 - 34 are related to possible **Chaos Issues**
Answers 35 - 45 are related to possible **Dysfunctional Issues**
Answers 46 - 54 are related to possible **Environmental Issues**

While this list of categories and issues is far from complete, I just wanted to demonstrate some of the most common issues and/or ways they can show up as part of a pattern. For now, I just want to get them on your radar as potential avenues of growth. We will get into working on the specific issues in subsequent chapters. The first step is always awareness and that's a big step. You're right on track so don't worry. We've got this.

Now, let's add up your answers and then take a look to see how they fit into the general categories. As an example, go back over your answers and every time you circled or checked off any number between 1 and 16, count that as one instance and write it down with the category. So, if you used any number in the range 42 times, write the number 42 next to the heading Abandonment Issues and repeat that process for each of the categories that begin with the letters A-E.

Remember to also use the denominator we arrived at earlier to reflect the number of scenarios used to arrive at your numbers. In our example above, we came up with the number 7 by adding 1 childhood scenario with 6 past partner scenarios. Once you're finished adding up your numbers, it may look something like this:

Abandonment Issues:	42/7
Bullying Issues:	39/7
Chaos Issues:	27/7
Dysfunctional Issues:	54/7
Environmental Issues:	12/7

Obviously, it stands to reason that the higher the number, the more pertinent the issue for you personally. Lower numbers may not be relevant or require any further consideration. For now, I just want you to be aware of the issue. In this example, Abandonment and Bullying issues seem to be prevalent so that is where you will focus your efforts going forward with the exercises. Here's a breakdown of the five different categories and what their organization means for you.

Abandonment Issues

When I clustered the answers of 1 - 16 together, I did that to represent some of the many scenarios that one may not directly associate with issues of abandonment but when taken together, begin to reveal a possible theme of what Abandonment might look like in the real world. For instance, if someone experienced a parent's (1) Divorce or (2) Separation or any other pattern of issues that led to the absence of a key individual or people, it might set in motion a pattern of seemingly unrelated events that all actually relate, directly or indirectly, to a pattern of abandonment. Consider how these events might mirror that issue: (3) Death, (4) Incarceration, (5) Drug rehab, (6) Custody disputes, (7) Family disputes, (8) Adoption, (9) Isolation, (10) Rejection, (11) Long distance romance, (12) Military service, (13) Job transfer, (14) Ghosted, (15) Sustained infrequent contact, or (16) Non-payment of support.

In isolation, these situations have no meaning other than the meaning given to them. When they begin to show up in a clear, convincing pattern, perhaps it warrants further scrutiny.

Bullying Issues

When I clustered the answers of 17 - 24 together, I did that to represent some of the many scenarios that one may not directly associate with issue of bullying but when taken together, begin to reveal a possible theme of what bullying behaviors might look like in the real world. For instance, if someone experienced a parent's (17) Domestic violence, (21) Name calling or any other pattern of behavior that encouraged bullying, it might set in motion seemingly unrelated events that all actually relate, directly or indirectly, to accepted bullying. Consider how these events might mirror that issue: (18) Cyberbullying, (19) Humiliation, (20) Objectification, (22) Personal attacks, (23) Verbal threats, or (24) Intimidation.

In isolation, these situations have no meaning other than the meaning given to them. When they begin to show up in a clear convincing pattern, perhaps it warrants further scrutiny.

Chaos Issues

When I clustered the answers of 25 - 34 together, I did that to represent some of the many scenarios that one may not directly associate with issue of chaos but when taken together, begin to reveal a possible theme of what chaotic behaviors might look like in the real world. For instance, if someone experienced a parent's (34) Substance abuse, (25) Manipulation or any other pattern of behavior that were chaotic and unsettling, it might set in motion seemingly unrelated events that all actually relate, directly or indirectly, to a pattern of behaviors that will constantly disrupt and cause trouble in relationships. Consider how these events might mirror that issue: (26) Injustice, (27) Shame. (28) Betrayal, (29) Exploitation, (30) Massive uncertainty, (31) Distant/disinterested, (32) Gossiping or (33) Spreading lies or innuendo.

In isolation, these situations have no meaning other than the meaning given to them. When they begin to show up in a clear, convincing pattern, perhaps it warrants further scrutiny.

Dysfunctional Issues

When I clustered the answers of 35 - 45 together, I did that to represent some of the many scenarios that one may not directly associate with dysfunctional family habits but when taken together, begin to reveal a possible theme of what those types of behaviors might look like in the real world. For instance, if someone experienced a parent's (36) Mental illness, (38) Addictions or any other pattern of behavior that were highly disruptive and unsustainable, it might set in motion seemingly unrelated events that all actually relate, directly or indirectly, to massive dysfunction. Consider how these events might mirror that issue: (35) Sexual assault, (37) Assault and battery, (39) Neglect, (40) Emotional abuse, (41) Narcissism, (42) Personality disorder, (43) Rage/anger issues, (44) Communication issues or (45) Promiscuity/cheating.

In isolation, these situations have no meaning other than the meaning given to them. When they begin to show up in a clear, convincing pattern, perhaps it warrants further scrutiny.

Environmental Issues

When I clustered the answers of 46 - 54 together, I did that to represent some of the many scenarios that one may not directly associate with environmental issues in the home but when taken together, begin to reveal a possible theme of what familial upheaval might look like in the real world. For instance, if someone experienced a parent's (46) Eviction, or were removed from the home involuntarily and put into (48) Foster care, or any other pattern of behavior that led to massive uncertainty and displacement, it might set in motion a pattern of seemingly unrelated events that all actually relate, directly or indirectly, to environmental insecurity. Consider how these events might mirror that issue: (47) Adoption, (49) Step-parents, (50) Accidents, (51) Fire, (52) Floods, (53) Natural disasters or (54) War/terror

In isolation, these situations have no meaning other than the meaning given to them. When they begin to show up in a clear, convincing pattern, perhaps it warrants further scrutiny.

One More Thing

Before we move on from this topic, I want to give you one other quick gift to consider. Up until now, I've been asking these questions from the perspective of what did YOU experience in your childhood and in your previous partnerships. That is exceptionally valuable information, especially when you crunch the numbers as I've demonstrated and begin to see the patterns that are there. Whether you had no clue at all about this, or you had a bit of an inkling, or you now know with even more clarity what you knew previously, this is important. I want you to have one more gift before we move on to other powerful exercises and it comes down to one simple question.

What Was Your Role in That?

Since I've created this checklist of behaviors to grade everyone else, maybe it's a great idea to do a little self-evaluation to determine if there are any areas that you may need or want to improve? Take this quick opportunity to go through my list one more time and see if there are any issues you'd like to improve for yourself. Of course, some of these won't apply at all because they were designed to show cross-contextual ways the five different themes show up and cause problems. I intentionally masked them among some other bad habits or sabotaging behaviors that ruin relationships. So, let's take one more look before we move on to see if there are some areas where the high performer in you may

Identifying Recurring Patterns

Circle THE NUMBER of any experience below that applies to you:

(1) Divorce

(2) Separation

(3) Death

(4) Incarceration

(5) Drug rehab

(6) Infidelity

(7) Family / Custody disputes

(8) Adoption

(9) Isolation

(10) Rejection

(11) Long distance romance

(12) Military service

(13) Job transfer

(14) Ghosted

(15) Sustained infrequent contact

(16) Non-payment of support

(17) Domestic violence

(18) Cyberbullying

(19) Humiliation

(20) Objectification

(21) Name calling

(22) Criticism / attacks

(23) Verbal threats

(24) Intimidation

(25) Manipulation

(26) Injustice

(27) Shame

(28) Betrayal

(29) Exploitation

(30) Massive uncertainty

(31) Distant / disinterested

(32) Gossiping

(33) Spreading lies or innuendo

(34) Substance abuse

(35) Sexual assault

(36) Mental illness

(37) Assault & battery

(38) Addictions

(39) Neglect

(40) Emotional abuse

(41) Narcissism

(42) Personality disorders

(43) Rage / anger issues

(44) Communication issues

(45) Promiscuity cheating

(46) Eviction

(47) Adoption

(48) Foster care

(49) Step-parents

(50) Accidents

(51) Fire

(52) Floods

(53) Natural disasters

(54) War / terror

want to up their game. Maybe you've engaged in (6) Infidelity in the past and you just want to commit to taking that off the table for you in the future based on principle. That would be huge. Or maybe you know you've engaged in (21) Name calling in the past and you just want to commit to not doing that because you know how much you hate it when someone does that to you. That would be a wonderful commitment. Perhaps you see that you may have inadvertently engaged in (14) Ghosting by just fading away over time and you want to be more resolute in your (44) Communication when you don't see a future with someone you've dated. The point is, high-value people get to be high-value by setting high standards for themselves. If that becomes one of your takeaways from this book, I honor you and salute your willingness to own your own role in any past challenges and commit to changing your own behavior.

What's one commitment you'd like to unilaterally claim as a way to improve how you show up in relationship?

_____

_____

Chapter 7:

Uncover Your Soul Messenger Matrix:

Freedom Awaits in Your H.E.A.R.T.™

 Since we want to heal the wounds and issues that are holding you back from finding and having the love you desire and deserve, we first have to identify the challenges. The problem with doing that is that oftentimes, those specific issues tend to linger beneath your conscious awareness, so they remain out of sight and out of mind. We've already begun to identify some of those possible recurring issues to consider in the previous Chapter and I helped you organize them into categories from A through E including Abandonment, Bullying, Chaos, Dysfunction or Environmental issues. In this Chapter, you'll discover another exercise designed to go even deeper to elicit the origins of even more of those hidden, deeply-rooted and unresolved issues. This is where the critical work of awareness comes into view.

It's kind of like when you brush up against a rough spot in wood and get a splinter or if you have a hangnail and it gets caught on your silk skirt. It's only through contact with something or someone else that the condition is revealed and brought to your conscious attention. From there, you can now address the situation and remedy it by smoothing out any rough spots. It's the same way with your personal "rough spots," also known as wounds.

Your personal wounds tend to be pretty stealthy and hard to spot until they get revealed by intimate contact with another. When you live alone or aren't being triggered by the conduct and actions of another, those issues just tend to lie dormant and waiting for the right conditions to be triggered. In other words, you can forget all about how your ex used to disrespect your time and show up late years ago until someone new starts exhibiting their own time management issues. Of course, their lateness might not have anything to do with you. It might be legitimate or job-related, but how well you handle it will absolutely reveal how well you healed it previously. Often, my clients would tell me their old issues had been healed and cleansed because they no longer even think about them and yet as soon as the conditions that created them get simulated, BAM! They pop right up like an old friend you're not exactly happy to see. In other words, one minute you're happy and content and then as soon as someone says something, or doesn't say something, or does something, or doesn't do something, you instantly get a rush of emotion that reminds you that a certain issue you thought was resolved is actually right there waiting for you.

So, if that's the case, what's the solution? Do you constantly have to get into new relationships, get the rug pulled out from under you at the worst possible time and then find yourself back at square one when it all goes badly, yet again? I know people who have done exactly that for years and even decades. There has got to be a better way than that.

Luckily for you, there *is* a better way to identify those lingering patterns of hurt. This is a powerful device I use to dig out unresolved issues so we can work with them. Just like weeds in a garden of beauty, it's a tremendous waste of time and energy to continually pull the tops off the weeds and try to keep them hidden out of sight. The reality is that those same weeds practically re-grow overnight and they are right back in place and on display for all the world to see by the light of day the next morning. That's why, if you're going to get rid of weeds, you have to pull them out by the R.O.O.T.s, otherwise, this tedious exercise becomes the ultimate fool's errand.

So, What *Is* This Better Way?

I created The Soul Messenger Matrix when I was inspired by the work of Imago therapy founders Harville Hendrix, Ph.D. and Helen LaKelly Hunt, Ph.D. The word Imago is Latin for image. It refers to the mold in which we developed in our formative years. That mold, along with some outstanding communication techniques, forms many of the underlying principles of Imago. With this basis, I began to develop my own methodology which I will teach here. Our parents and caretakers literally molded us either in their image or in the image they wanted us to take on consciously or unconsciously.

The word matrix is an English word that actually refers to the form which creates a molded product. It's the pattern which shapes, contours and creates an exact replica of the same product again and again whether it's a plastic bottle or a clamshell casing used in custom packaging. What's interesting about this metaphor is that in an industrial environment, a precision matrix or mold will reliably and without fail create and recreate the exact product with precision every single time. That's the power of precision calibration, machining and control of all outside influences like raw material, ingredients, temperature, centrifugal force, etc. However, in a human, the process of molding has far too many uncontrollable influences to accurately create and recreate the very same "product" again and again. There are too many uncontrollable factors and variables. Because humans have free will and complex nervous systems, they are unpredictable. They can decide what things mean. They have natural interests and abilities. They can be influenced by outside sources. That's why two children, twins even, can be raised in the exact same conditions and grow up to become polar opposites. One can be troubled, and one can be a model citizen. One could be a gifted athlete, the other not so much. There's something powerful in the human spirit that can be influenced, but it's very hard to control reliably over time and with variables. The good news is that since you're reading this book and doing these powerful exercises, you are influencing the precise variables that will make all the difference in the world for you.

First, A Word of Warning

Before I introduce the assessment, I want to caution you, in advance, to prepare and inform you. I recently had one client tell me the assessment didn't resonate for her at all, despite the fact that every single situation she shared came directly from her own mouth and experience. Interestingly enough, though, one of the things we had to work on with her was her habitual default of running a "mis-matcher" pattern. People navigate the world and make decisions on what things mean using their own unique filters on the world that are created by past experience. These filters are called meta-programs in the science of Neuro-Linguistic Programming. Usually these meta-programs are revealed in the reflexive habits of the individual.

Most people would tend to default to either a matcher or a mis-matcher strategy. Matchers reflexively work to build rapport with others by looking for commonalities that connect. For instance, they'll comment on your clothing and say they have a very similar shirt just like that. Or they'll find out where you went on vacation and offer up that they've been there too and loved it. Matchers seek to connect by "sorting through sameness."

On the other hand, "mis-matchers" don't sort by sameness. They "sort by difference" and look for the incongruities and outliers. They actually feel significant by showing how smart and perceptive they are by identifying how a pattern doesn't match. These people are born proofreaders, inspectors, detectives, compliance managers, maybe even comedians, and they are very good at what they do, but it can come at a cost in their relationships. They're great at finding what's wrong or doesn't match. It's one thing to do that to objects on an assembly line or characters in a line of text. It's another thing entirely to do that to human beings.

Imagine what it's like for the child who comes home from school proud of the "A" on their test, only to be quizzed by a mis-matcher parent on why they got a "95" instead of a "100." Maybe you know what that's like and don't have to imagine it. It's crushing when it happens over and over again. That's what it's like to be in a relationship with a mis-matcher because you just can't ever win. It's problematic to say the least for the other people around them.

Here's the reality: that which matches, and that which doesn't match, is *always* available. That is literally indicative of the concept of balance. I teach my clients that you will always find whatever you look for, so I suggest people look for what's great in their partner. Yes, I know they're not perfect, but if you look for what's great or what you admire about them, you'll find it and you'll both feel good. If you look for how they're not good enough, you'll find that, too. Then both of you will feel miserable. That doesn't sound very smart at all, does it? That's why it's so important for people to mitigate their old mis-matcher tendencies and balance it out with some matcher strategies.

The good news is that once I honed in on this particular client's mis-matcher tendencies, I was able to show her why her relationships and health were both struggling. Yes, being a mis-matcher in all situations is physically exhausting and damaging to your health because it's just bad energy. There's one other reason this mis-matcher strategy is so devastating, especially in the realm of relationships: by "picking apart" and sitting in harsh judgment of intimate partners, relationships don't last. She will eventually end up with someone who's been so beaten down, she won't respect them, or she'll end up alone. Every. Single. Time. This habit, left unchecked, will only ever lead to misery, heartbreak and disappointment for her and others.

I believe people occasionally use this default response as a form of self-defense against vulnerability and to keep people or ideas at a distance. So, let me tell you in advance, if you find yourself having a similar response to this assessment as you take it, that's fine. I simply ask that you consider the above explanation and whether it is relevant to you. Could it be possible that your tendency to critique and look at what's wrong with nearly *everything* is at least part of your challenge?

This is too important to just block out and overlook and if it resonates at any level, I invite you to take a step back and at least consider how that learned habitual response might be sabotaging you in plain sight.

One More Word of Caution

While some may get a huge aha moment from this assessment that can change everything and some may dispute the relevance or accuracy altogether, there is one more possibility. Whatever you do, I urge you, *in advance,* not to use this new insight or information to feel bad, guilty or ashamed. This is also a bit of a default response based on habit and conditioning and I want to assure you there is NO value to be found in feeling that way. None. I don't share this to assign blame or shame. I share this in order to make the invisible visible, and help you identify the healing path forward. I share this because you *are* worthy of love no matter what happened to you in the past.

This diagnostic tool identifies what happened *to* you when you were an innocent child. You did not have the benefit of power to change anything at the time it was happening. In fact, you probably didn't even have enough awareness or ability to change anything. That's why I urge you not to re-victimize yourself all over again. It won't help in any way whatsoever and it will only rob you of perhaps your best chance ever to heal these lingering issues once and for all.

If you feel an instinct to double down on any shame or guilt that isn't yours to carry after all I've written, I highly recommend that you do an internal check-in to see why you may be knowingly and willingly choosing to self-sabotage and stay stuck right where you are, feeling bad. As a coach, I can tell you that it's not uncommon for people to choose "the devil they know" over the prospect of an unknown future, even if the future potential is bright and promising. When this happens, I am more than willing to lovingly challenge my clients in order to serve them. However, since this is a book and I'm not there to wrestle you down in person, I urge you to take full advantage of this opportunity in front of you right now. I promise you that the freedom and potential for joy and healing is so much better than the prison of your own making that you're considering. Just don't do it. Repeat after me: IT WAS NOT MY FAULT. There is no value or purpose in continuing to punish yourself.

Into the Matrix

I am going to give you five questions, and an acronym to help you with the process. That acronym is the word H.E.A.R.T. because it's extremely easy to remember and that is specifically where the answers reside that will set you free. All you need to do is follow my five simple questions and go where they want to lead you. I strongly urge you to take a few moments and give yourself the gift of answering these five simple questions *before* you read further. It will only take a few minutes but the answers you harvest could literally save you years and decades of struggle if you follow my directions and give yourself this gift. When you do this correctly, your answers just may reveal some powerful, provocative clues that could change *everything* for you. At the same time, if you ignore my strong suggestion and read on before you answer five simple questions, I have to ask where else you might be self-sabotaging by trying to know all the answers without doing the work? Three of the costliest and most dangerous words in the English language are "I know that" and they will keep you stuck. Do yourself a favor and accept the gift I'm giving you. You have nothing to lose and everything to gain so let's get started.

Two Simple Rules

The following five questions should be answered from the perspective of your own childhood eyes in the first seven years of your life. Think of what you saw as a child. Remember what you felt. Revisit your experiences and learnings as a young child before your eighth birthday. If you have no recollection at all, or if you're not sure, do your best to imagine what you think it might have been and give yourself permission to just write down whatever comes to mind. Trust your intuition and don't try to filter the answer in any way. In fact, write down the very first thing that comes to mind. Even if your brain tells you, "no that's not right," definitely write it down. Just trust that there's no such thing as a wrong answer and go with whatever comes up; we'll figure out the rest of it later.

Second, as you answer the questions, most may likely refer to memories of your parents because they are oftentimes the primary influencers and caretakers. Of course, one size does not necessarily fit all, so whether it's about parents, family members, foster parents, clergy, day care providers or whomever had an influential effect in your youth, write the answer that comes to mind and simply note where the experience originated. Are you ready? Turn the page and begin now. Whatever you do...

...DO NOT MOVE ON TO THE NEXT CHAPTER UNTIL YOU ANSWER THE QUESTIONS!

The Soul Messenger Matrix
Simply follow your H.E.A.R.T. to where *freedom* awaits!

The H stands for HURTS

1. Name three childhood HURTS, disappointments or negative traits of the people who raised you. This might include traits like critical, unavailable, abusive or any number of possibilities.

1)
2)
3)
Extra credit answers:
4)
5)

The E stands for EMPATHIC EXPECTATIONS or EMOTIONS

2. In regard to the three childhood HURTS listed above, what did you hope for instead? This would most likely be the opposite of your answers to the question above and may include answers like safe, good enough, loved, etc.

1)
2)
3)
Extra credit answers:
4)
5)

The A stands for ASSUMPTIONS

3. As a result of those three childhood HURTS in the first question, what ASSUMPTIONS did you make about yourself and your own value or inherent worth in light of those hurts? Some possible answers might include that you weren't good or smart

enough, you were the wrong body weight, not attractive enough, etc.

1)
2)
3)
Extra credit answers:
4)
5)

The R stands for REACTIONS

4. As a result of those three childhood HURTS from the first question, and any other frustrations, how did you REACT or respond and what patterns of behavior showed up when you felt that way? For instance, did you retreat and get quiet, yell, act destructively or self-harm? Write down whatever you recall.

1)
2)
3)
Extra credit answers:
4)
5)

The T stands for TRIGGERS

5. As a result of those three childhood HURTS from the first question, what actions or patterns demonstrated by others TRIGGER those old wounds and create an emotional reaction? Some possible answers might include criticism, being ignored, getting yelled at, disrespected or a range of other possibilities.

1)
2)
3)
Extra credit answers:
4)
5)

Chapter 8:

Into the Matrix-Revealed:
New Awareness for Old Issues

 The Soul Messenger Matrix is a series of five simple and very short questions that allows one to laser focus on precisely what unfinished business from childhood may remain to be healed. I find it pretty brilliant because it's a sneak peek into the space between your expectations and your experience. In that very fertile space between those two points, you will find clues regarding childhood wounds. Some may have been addressed. Others, as I said earlier, may be lying in wait, only to be triggered when the circumstances of a situation align somewhat with a wound you haven't addressed yet. That's what we refer to as "unfinished business."

The Map and the Territory

In the practice of NLP or Neuro-Linguistic Programming, we explore the linkages between language or verbiage and the coding that processes, stores and retrieves information in the human nervous system. We have a common axiom in NLP circles that addresses the discrepancy between what I earlier framed as expectations and experiences. In NLP, we say that "when the map doesn't match the territory, the territory is always right." The territory actually refers to the land beneath your feet, which can't be wrong because it's reality. The tree to your right is real whether it shows up on your map or not. A map is simply a visual representation of that actual land. It can be skewed entirely by the power of perspective and the perception of the viewer. It is also subject to change because any map is a reflection of a moment in time. Take a look at any photo or map of your home town from 100 years ago and then try to use it to navigate. It would be a challenge since the old horse feed store may have long ago given way to condominiums. Or the house you grew up in may have once been virgin forest. The reality here is that time marches on and things change whether you like it, realize it or even notice it. Change is the one constant because everything changes. Another way to frame this concept is the blueprint and the building. Just because an architect used his imagination to add skylights to his design doesn't mean they won't get cut out due to a budget over-run and never see "the light of day." Bottom line, there's probably a million reasons why expectations and the experience or execution don't match up in the end.

Whether you're talking about an actual map or building, discrepancies may cause inconvenience or frustration, but they seldom rise to level of causing psychological pain or discomfort unless they result in some type of a dispute or a legal proceeding. However, when you focus on the discrepancy between a human's expectations and their experiences, especially at such a tender age and foundational stage, that dichotomy between what you wanted and what you perceive you got is the root of the pain.

Now to be fair, if you knew how those issues were affecting you today, you almost certainly would have addressed them. However, in order to address those R.O.O.T. issues, you'd have to identify them and make them both visible and tangible. So, let's get right to it and identify the hidden wounds obscured by your current perception.

Follow the H.E.A.R.T. Assessment

Each letter in the H.E.A.R.T. acronym shared in the previous chapter corresponds to one specific aspect of your childhood experience. As you may expect or know very well from your own experience, most adults seldom give much conscious thought or attention to events from the distant past deemed irrelevant and largely unimportant. As a rule, we tend to drive forward by looking through the windshield instead of the rear-view mirror. That's usually a great idea but if we fail to harvest the lessons and gifts of the past, we can lose them entirely. That would be really unfortunate because there are valuable learnings and lessons that came to serve you. I'm really clear that the past does not equal the future unless you live there. However, when you fail to get the lessons from the past that you need, you will get them served up again. As a result, my recommendation is that you live an examined life where you move toward consciousness and enlightenment to the degree you can whenever possible.

By considering each of those key areas in the context I've suggested, I'm going to help reveal information from your past that is most likely largely hidden from your top-of-mind awareness and still absolutely relevant to today. Just because you're not consciously aware of it or thinking about how it may be affecting you *still* every single day, doesn't mean it's not happening. By directing you where to look and asking a specific question, I've essentially given you a map to buried treasure, pointed out the "X" that marks the spot where you want to dig and handed you a shovel. I hope you took that opportunity to do a little digging because just like a treasure map, there are definite rewards ahead for those who do the work. This is your very last chance to answer those questions before we move ahead and reveal what you need to know. If you picked up this book because you want to live your best life and enjoy great relationships, flip back a few pages and write down your answers now. Better yet, write your answers in the *Companion. Peace.* workbook that I mentioned in an earlier Chapter and created to go with this book as a companion piece.

Question Number One Revealed

In the H.E.A.R.T. acronym revealed in the previous chapter, the assignment for question number one was for you to identify the letter H which stood for the HURTS or disappointments from your childhood:

Name three childhood HURTS or negative traits of the people who raised you.

Once you identify your answers, we plug them into the following key:

Believe it or not, I am actually attracted to someone who is:_____,_____**and**

_____.

Yes, that's right. The great irony is that we have an invisible attraction to the very thing we hated. Doesn't that start to immediately explain exactly why your previous relationships haven't worked out the way you wanted them to feel? Now can you start to see why your previous relationships may have been attainable, yet never sustainable? It almost boggles the mind! You have to ask yourself, "If I hated this as a child, when I was powerless to change it, why on earth would I continue making the same poor choices when I *finally* have the power to make a better choice?"

Remember: it's not because you are crazy or a glutton for punishment, or somehow bad or undeserving. You don't even consciously realize you're doing it! It's just that we all have to act out love's little three-act play, also known as the three-stage healing process that I shared earlier. It goes like this:

1) We get wounded in our relationships.
2) Then we get triggered in our relationships.
3) And ultimately, we get healed in our relationships.

Just to be clear, in that third stage, healing can't happen until we finally get the lessons and resolve them for good. The challenge with a child at the tender age of under seven years old is that they are, by definition, myopic and think the world revolves around them. Perhaps, in an ideal world, it should. But, alas, it's not an ideal world, far from it sometimes.

Look at a few examples from my clients and see if this makes sense:

- My client, Melinda, was actually attracted to someone who was <u>emotionally unavailable</u>, <u>lazy</u>, <u>unmotivated and accepted no responsibility</u>. Hmm, I wonder why that's not working out?

- My client, Sharon, was actually attracted to someone who was <u>controlling</u>, <u>bossy</u>, <u>opinionated</u> and <u>critical</u>. Well guess what? She found him. And divorced him, too! Surprise, surprise.

- My client, Elaine, was actually attracted to someone who <u>had impossible standards</u>, <u>was unpredictable</u> and <u>distant</u>. Is it any wonder that Elaine avoids relationships and sees them as a place of nothing but pain while staying busy with work?

- My client, Tammy, was actually attracted to someone who <u>ignored her</u>, <u>paid no attention to her</u> and <u>had no backbone</u>. Would you believe her partner has learned to ignore the problems he knows he can't fix, staying busy elsewhere working away from home and being kind of wishy-washy at making decisions? What are the odds, right?

Well if you're finding this enlightening so far, wait until you get to Question number two and you **really** start to see the challenge.

Question Number Two Revealed

In the H.E.A.R.T. acronym revealed in the previous chapter, the assignment for question number two was for you to identify the letter E which stood for the EMPATHIC EXPECTATIONS from your childhood, also known as what you wanted **instead** of those primary HURTS from question one.

In regard to the three childhood HURTS,
what did you hope for instead?

Once you identify your answers, we plug them into the following key:

Although you really hope he or she will be: _____,
_____ and _____.

This question comes right after question one and we finally see the impossibly maddening duality that we can never achieve. To really drive this point home, imagine that while you're invisibly attracted to the very worst traits of your childhood caretakers, you are *simultaneously* hoping that they will model the exact opposite trait instead. To make matters even more frustrating, most of the time, your parents **absolutely** demonstrated those traits you hoped for in other contexts or times. For instance, most-of-the-time critical parents were also complimentary at times. Abusive parents could be kind and affectionate. Absent parents have a knack for trying to make up for their absence by being very present or generous, even if it seems to be a fleeting gift. That's exactly what causes some of our confusion, mixed messages and uncertain expectations.

Let's take a look at those previous examples of my clients that I showed you earlier:

- While my client, Melinda, was actually attracted to someone who was emotionally unavailable, she secretly hoped they'll be dependable. How might that be possible?!? Simultaneously, despite her attraction to someone who's lazy and unmotivated, she silently hopes they'll be hard-working. Lastly, while she has been attracted to people who accepted no responsibility, her secret hope was that they'd be loyal! (While this isn't an exact opposite, in this particular case, it is what she filled in on her form. I know she also wanted her parent to be responsible). This is what creates the incredible confusion and frustration; what you want and what you get are, oftentimes, polar opposites! Knowing what you know so far, what kind of odds would you give on that happening? It would probably be a long shot, right? *This* is why she's struggled. It also may explain exactly why *you* have struggled as well. And this only covers two of the five questions I asked in the Soul Messenger Matrix. Let's continue the examples:

- My client, Sharon, was unaware that she was actually attracted to someone who was <u>controlling and bossy,</u> but she held out hope that he'd be <u>stable (which is how she languages what she wanted instead. It's not an exact opposite in this case but we can infer that she believes a stable parent wouldn't be controlling or bossy)</u>. Then while she was attracted to a man who was <u>extremely opinionated</u>, she hoped simultaneously that he would be a <u>good listener!</u> How does that happen?! Then, finally, her invisible connection to a <u>critical partner</u> made her long for one who was also <u>fair</u>. Can you see how incongruent those traits are and what a long-shot it might be for that to work out?

- My client, Elaine, was actually unknowingly attracted to someone who had <u>impossible standards,</u> but she also hoped he would *have* <u>high standards!</u> That's literally like looking for the one needle in the haystack that would stick you! Then she was also magnetically drawn to a partner who was <u>unpredictable,</u> but she hoped he'd be <u>loyal</u>. Hmm, I'd consider that somewhat risky. If that's not threading the needle too much, she also wanted a man who was simultaneously <u>distant</u> and <u>hard working</u>. Again, while that's not an exact opposite in this case, it does pretty much guarantee she'll fall in love with someone who may travel just as much as she does and never commits to love! Can you see this?

- My client, Tammy, was actually unaware that she was attracted to someone who <u>ignored her and paid no attention to her,</u> but her secret yearning was to simultaneously <u>feel loved and important</u>. That might be somewhat challenging at best, impossible at worst. At the same time, she's attracted to partners who <u>had no backbone</u> but somehow, they should be <u>resolute and self-assured</u> enough to be able to make her <u>feel special</u>. How do you think her guy was doing? Not so well.

Can you see how nearly impossible this all gets when we compound these invisible drives with these conscious hopes simultaneously? It gives a whole new meaning to the term "opposites attract!"

Question Number Three Revealed

In the H.E.A.R.T. acronym revealed in the previous chapter, the assignment for question number three was for you to identify the letter A which stood for the ASSUMPTIONS from your childhood that you may have made about yourself as a result of those primary hurts listed in question number one.

What ASSUMPTIONS did you make about yourself and your own value or inherent worth in light of those hurts?

Once you identify your answers, we plug them into the following key:

Because the truth is, these are the roots of your greatest fears _____.

Question number three reveals the seeds planted in your formative years that grow the basis of your greatest fears, and they don't typically just disappear overnight. In fact, they tend to lay there dormant just waiting to be activated all over again in adulthood and beyond. It's also very important to remember that these don't necessarily have to be true or have a real basis in fact. These are the thoughts of a child regarding their deepest fears and potential risks. Basically, what happens is that when a child gets hurt by some kind of action, word or deed, he or she tends to make an assumption about *why*, specifically, that happened. It's like an investigator looking for clues at the scene of the crime. Since a child is hardly a seasoned investigator, the clues they "discover" may be somewhat misleading because they were found and viewed through the prism of their own hurts, disappointments and wounding. Quite simply, a child's lack of perspective and world experience already makes their investigatory skills suspect, and that gets even more complicated when what they see gets filtered through their own unique bias.

For instance, when a child feels like they can never be good enough in some way, the upside is that it may drive them to achieve but the downside is that it can make them absolutely paranoid about what will happen if somehow they *don't* meet expectations. You can expect that "fear of not measuring up" to continue well into adulthood and show up in multiple ways. Children who are shamed over their weight tend to be very sensitive to body issues their whole lives and it can show up in a variety of ways. Children with absentee or unavailable parents tend to fear that it was their own imagined inferior worth that led to them feeling rejected or abandoned when it was actually their parent's issues that had nothing to do with them. If a child is made to feel like they have to be smart in order to be loved, they will likewise have a tremendous fear of being revealed as "not smart enough" and that will cause them to be hyper-vigilant regarding ways that can possibly occur. Over time, that vigilance distorts because we have to find what we look for so eventually, they will discover ways that they fear will make them look "stupid" that have nothing whatsoever to do with intelligence. Pretty soon, that exaggerated fear becomes a self-fulfilling prophecy resulting in all-new and totally irrelevant, unfair examples that the individual will fear proves them stupid, when, in fact, it does not.

When you pull away all the various ways an adult can have a sensitivity to somehow not being good enough, it will usually lead directly to one or more of the big four emotions as it spirals downward. It may create a great deal of **shame** and a fear of being revealed. It could spark some **guilt** over what may have been done or not done. It might even lead to an even deeper fear of **rejection** for not being good enough which then oftentimes spirals down even further to a fear of **abandonment**. The really corrosive thing about this spiraling downward process is that what usually starts with the primary fear of not feeling good enough in some way leads to the secondary fear that as a result, you also won't be loved. Ultimately, when that spiraling process continues even further, it can lead directly to base survival because if you're not enough and won't be loved, the next assumption is that you may as well be dead. Obviously, this is a very dangerous and unnecessary spiral. It becomes particularly important to understand those little forgotten fears and assumptions that were planted as seeds long ago, tend to take root and grow over time. By bringing your attention back to these stealthy stories, I want to create a new awareness and from there, ultimately give you the tools to heal them.

So, here's how this worked for some of my clients that you're getting to know by now:

- My client, Melinda, assumed that she <u>didn't belong in her own family</u> and was <u>never accepted for who she was</u> due to her mom's emotional distance and her father's absence after their divorce. In fact, after her mother kicked her out, her fear was that she would be <u>rejected and abandoned</u> if she ever revealed who she was and how she felt. I covered this pattern more in-depth in Chapter 5. Unfortunately, this fear has created a recurring pattern of experiencing rejection and abandonment, which I've helped her see. She has a lot of ways to fear that she won't be accepted and that's why she's attracted those very scenarios. Again, these new awareness's that reveal lessons are not to torture you. They're happening to heal you.

- My client, Sharon, had a similar answer for different reasons. Her mom was a school teacher who highly valued order and discipline. They made her assume and fear that <u>love and approval might be taken away if she wasn't perfect</u>. Her mom ran a pretty tight ship and didn't accept any nonsense or back talk. Her assumption was that she <u>had to be perfect to be good enough</u>. To an impressionable young girl, that came across as

101

pretty controlling and critical. While an orderly household is a great thing, the downside of strong authoritarian tendencies is that there is at least an implied punishment, and usually an applied one. Occasionally, it can be harsh which only complicates things. In this case, Sharon's familiarity with criticism made her a perfect target for the narcissist she eventually married. One of her biggest concerns and fears is that she's "not doing it right" and might be wrong. This occasionally makes it very difficult to take action or assume risks and it's possibly even contributed to a physical disability that limits her activities. The good news is that the excellent progress she has made in some very key areas have improved her quality of life a great deal.

- My client, Elaine, also had parents with impossible standards who were unpredictable and distant, so her assumption was that <u>she had to be quite an over-achiever to get and hold their attention</u>. However, she's far more driven by fear and a desire to please than excellence, which meets her desire to attract attention via achievement. Plus, her parent's work ethic has made her subordinate any desires or dreams of her own in order to stay in a job that requires a great deal of travel and nearly unsustainable working conditions. She learned unconsciously at a very early age that she was <u>expected to fulfill other people's expectations rather than her own</u>. She understands this trade-off and for now, she is more driven by the status quo, her finances and work she knows versus an unknown future with no other guarantees. At some point, that could change but for now, she has gotten somewhat comfortable in her discomfort.

- My client, Tammy, had a history of feeling ignored and unimportant, unless she was getting spanked for misbehaving. Ironically, while getting spanked was painful and unpleasant, she learned to prefer it because in some way, it hurt less than the pain of being ignored. Her assumption was that since she wasn't getting attention without conflict; conflict equaled attention. Still, today, she uses conflict and arguments as a way to connect with her partner when she's not getting his attention. The bad news is, for him, conflict doesn't connect them; it drives the wedge even further that pushes him away. Plus, while she didn't feel like she got emotional connection, in her childhood, wealth was valued. So, now, in some ways, she equates money with love and attention. As a result of the difficulties in her relationship, she has found other ways to meet her needs for attention including her very impressive art and her beautiful children. While she's found reliable vehicles to get the attention she craves, she still longs to feel loved, important and special. When she does not get these desired feelings, those stubborn assumptions made by her as a little girl can still create pain and bring out a side of her she'd rather not feel.

Question Number Four Revealed

In the H.E.A.R.T. acronym revealed in the previous chapter, the assignment for question number four was for you to identify the letter R which stood for the REACTIONS from your childhood. The idea here is to learn how exactly you tended to respond as a child when frustrated.

As a result of those three childhood hurts and any other frustrations, how did you REACT and what patterns of behavior showed up when you were frustrated?

Once you identify your answers, we plug them into the following key:

Ironically, you sabotage and prevent yourself from getting the kind of love you want by _____.

In question number four, we get back to perhaps the most intriguing turnaround in this diagnostic tool because it's actually such a powerful wake-up call. That's because it demonstrates loud and clear where and how, exactly, people go wrong when it comes to finding the kind of love they so richly deserve. Once people hone in on their precise strategy for dealing with frustration, they see immediately why their tactics never work. They didn't work in childhood, they don't work in adulthood either. Moody sulking. Silent treatments. Disappearing acts. Self-soothing or self-medicating. Passive-aggressive challenges. Rage storms. Destructive tendencies. Slamming doors. Throwing objects. Violent attacks. Angry outbursts. Temper tantrums. Name calling. Making accusations. Self-harm. Whether people run for cover and hide out or they ramp it up for effect, these techniques simply aren't very effective when it comes to getting a loving response.

Conspicuously absent in these ineffective approaches are the simple, reliable choices that _do_ work effectively time and time again. That's exactly what I teach my clients. I help them learn, know or remember their true value and self-worth. I help them stay grounded, and confident while embodying an unshakeable self-worth. I help them learn the powerful difference between making a request and issuing demands or edicts. I teach them how to speak their truth from an empowered place of clarity and decisiveness.

Perhaps most effective of all, I teach my clients that contrary to what they may have believed in the past, their vulnerability is not weakness by any stretch of the imagination. This is a common misperception. In fact, I'd dare say that anyone who thinks vulnerability is weakness has never stood in front of someone, laid down their weapons and defenses and just gotten nakedly authentic with what they desire. It's definitely not as easy as it sounds and it's definitely not for everybody. In fact, I show my clients the true power of vulnerability and raw authenticity when it comes to creating the kind of life and love of your dreams. It's not only powerful, I'd make the case that it's actually the magic power that brings out the very best in your partner. A little humility and kindness, combined with confidence, goes a very long way when it comes to getting a partner to reciprocate that kind of good will. You might even say, these traits described are the very essence of a loving response between intimate partners.

Let's revisit some of the excellent client examples I've been sharing in this Chapter:

- My client, Melinda, frequently <u>gave in and stayed quiet</u> for a very long time until she couldn't take it anymore and then she would <u>lash out and get angry</u> when she couldn't seem to get what she wanted. This is a common pattern for someone who lived in fear of expressing herself fully. She would bottle things up so much until the pressure built so high she would just explode, and that usually went very badly for her. That only exacerbated her fears since clamming up and blowing up are both terrible strategies that don't work. She now does a much better job of managing her emotions that used to get the best of her. Plus, she is much more strategic in the way she expresses herself under stress. For her, she is learning to quietly embody her true worth and ask for what she wants from an agreeable, confident and loving place

- My client, Sharon, would <u>retreat into her own world and avoid confrontations</u> she knew she couldn't win. She also tended to <u>check out into a bit of a fantasy world by burying her face in a book or watching TV for an escape</u>. Of course, she also learned the power of <u>self-medicating with food to change the way she felt in a given moment</u>. As some of you may know, that can be a learned behavior with some serious long-term consequences. With skills like those, she was a dream wife for the narcissist she married because he knew just how to keep her in check, until she started to learn a different strategy and finally broke away. We attract exactly what we need in order to grow, learn and heal. Once we do, a different reality is possible.

- My client, Elaine, also engaged in some withdrawing behaviors where she would often <u>read or just escape into a world of make-believe</u> that was cleverly concealed inside her bedroom closet. Still, today, these coping mechanisms show up in her love of travel and a desire to meet new people because she still seeks dependable ways to escape. As you might expect, checking out and avoiding any kind of relationship stress is not what I'd call a recommended tactic. When she's ready to change, she'll need to develop some more effective strategies in order to get what she wants.

- My client, Tammy, who craved attention when she felt she didn't matter had a habit of <u>acting out in an attempt to try to get what she wanted</u>. For her, conflict equaled connection because it was better than being ignored. Then, as she got older, she began to experiment with more defiant, higher-risk behaviors that created even more conflict. In her teens she began to <u>use drugs and sexuality to get what she wanted</u>, but that also created a fair amount of pain and disappointment for her as well. Sometimes, she got what she thought she wanted in the short term, but that strategy always seemed to fail miserably when it came to long term success.

As you can see, there are many ways to *attempt* to meet one's needs when it comes to experiencing love, but many of them simply don't work long-term or reliably. If you were to ask the clients whose stories I shared, they would probably agree, it wasn't for a lack of trying. The problem is, it doesn't matter how hard you try. The wrong strategy will always lead to the wrong response no matter how many times you attempt to make it work. I help my clients understand their old behaviors through the lens of a new filter and then I help them master better, more effective ways to get the love the want and deserve. I can help you do that here, too. Let's keep going.

Question Number Five Revealed

In the H.E.A.R.T. acronym revealed in the previous chapter, the assignment for question number five was for you to identify the letter T which stood for the TRIGGERS based on your childhood experiences.

As a result of your childhood hurts, what actions or patterns demonstrated by others TRIGGER those old assumptions and wounds that create an emotional reaction?

Once you identify your answers, we plug them into the following key:

Every time anything remotely like this happens, these are the things that will cause you a great deal of stress and possibly sabotage you until you heal them: _____.

Old wounds can be buried very deeply so it requires some real work to dig around and excavate them for your own good. That's why I want to be so sure to give you this awareness of what, specifically, you should be looking for before it gets triggered and self-sabotage takes over. The best way to find your triggers is to look for them in an un-triggered state. When you know very well what triggers you, you can anticipate it and catch it quickly. This new awareness is also one of the most important stages of healing.

Let me share with you perhaps one of the very best and most profound examples of a Trigger I've ever heard. Just last week, at a speaking engagement, one of the people attending my talk was sharing and asking questions about identifying triggers. I happened to know a little about his history because he had shared with me that he had lived on the streets, homeless, for more than a decade. As we spoke that day, we celebrated the fact that he had been clean, sober and off the streets for nearly two years. He had a great job with a lot of responsibility and was even in a relationship. He shared with me the devastating trajectory that led him to the one day, years into his homelessness, where he actually found himself doing what was once unthinkable. He described, in detail, the day where he found himself eating out of a trash can to survive. He told me about the homeless friend he learned to count on who would share his food with him. At the time he gratefully devoured the very welcome food, he had no idea it had also been salvaged from local dumpsters. He shared how when he first learned about his resourceful friend's strategy for finding food, he would wake up early, before sunrise, to do his own foraging. He was terrified of being seen doing it. Predictably, one day, his greatest fear materialized. He was spotted digging in a trash can by an old family friend because he was "living" not far from where he grew up, around friends and family. He said it was one of his absolute lowest and most shameful moments because he knew word would get back to his family.

Here's where the trigger part is relevant. As we were talking, he shared with me and the entire room that he could not stand to be yelled at because his mother yelled at him all the time as a child. His voice cracked as he recalled just how painful it was for him. He said he almost never yells at anyone because he hates it so much. He actually started to tear up and shake his head slightly as he recalled that the very few times he ever yelled in his life, he was crying so hard people could barely understand a word he was yelling. In that moment, the room was eerily quiet because we collectively felt the depth of that man's pain.

In a moment of clarity, I broke the silence in the room with the words, "Can I ask you a question?" My words pulled him out of his own painful trance, and he said, "Sure, you can ask me anything." Then I asked him what I pretty much already knew. I said, "Did your time on the street begin with someone yelling at you, just as you've described?" With a stunned silence and a nearly imperceptible head shake, he nodded affirmatively and the whole room simultaneously discovered just how powerful a trigger can be and how it can change a life in profound, and sometimes even permanent, way. This good, kind-hearted man was so tender and sensitive to being yelled at that he left his family to live on the street in absolute uncertainty and occasional terror for more than a decade. In fact, it hurt him so badly that he developed a devastating drug habit as a way to medicate the pain just to make it even remotely manageable for him. Triggers can be devastating. And by the way, most people have dozens, or hundreds of triggers embedded in their subconscious simultaneously. This is why this work, and this book, is so very important.

It takes considerable work to have someone trip one of your old triggers and instead of reacting angrily in a flash, you simply observe the feeling from a distance and evaluate it. By expecting it before it ever occurs, you can remove a great deal of the emotional charge that gets in the way of good decision-making. You can see it for what it is and *know* that it is happening to teach you, not torture you. This is when you are well on your way to healing and mastery.

In order to accurately crack the code on your personal triggers, you need to be able to use the H.E.A.R.T. acronym I've shared to reverse engineer some of your past upsets. Once you identify your Hurts, Empathic Expectations, Assumptions and Reactions, you have everything you need to ask the question, "What needs to happen in order for me to get triggered and upset?" Think back to some of the times when you've been most angry and ask yourself, what happened just before that to trigger that response? For some it might be getting ignored, passed over or dismissed. Maybe it's being disrespected or unappreciated. For some it could be getting insulted, yelled at or even physically attacked. There are all kinds of ways for this to happen and remember, these are custom designed for you based on your past history and experience. What makes one person triggered might make another laugh. It really is based on what happened to you in the past and the meaning you attached to it at the time.

- If you recall, my client, Melinda, has a few different triggers from her personal history. Some are just irritating while others might be immediate fight, flight or freeze generators. She knows one of her primary irritants occurs when she is feeling dismissed or ignored. When it escalates to yelling, demanding or ridicule, the intensity increases until it potentially culminates in a physical attack. She knows to be aware and vigilant any time those triggers get activated.

- My client, Sharon, identifies her triggers as criticism, name calling or taunting. Oftentimes, the insults are based on her intelligence, general abilities and even worth. Her biggest worry is simply being "good enough" in just about any endeavor. These were favorite targets of her ex-husband who as a narcissist, had an uncanny ability to identify any specific gaps in her self-worth. The good news is that she has come a long way in healing those wounds. It's worth remembering that it's a journey of healing and it takes time. It's not simply about the destination. The journey *is* the process of healing. You just have to start and stay on track.

- My client, Elaine, was also sensitive to simply being enough. She tends to get overwhelmed when she is over-worked and fatigued. She prefers complementary feedback and positive affirmation on a regular basis in order to feel accomplished. When that gets withheld, it only adds to her stress and insecurity. The problem is, when that happens, her first instinct is to double down which only exacerbates the whole cycle of fatigue. With this particular set of triggers, adrenal burnout is a potentially serious risk unless it gets identified and modified.

- My client, Tammy, gets triggered by <u>feeling ignored or not getting enough positive attention</u>. She also tends to react harshly when she sees someone who appears to be weak or spineless due to a parent who avoided conflict and stayed silent rather than defend her. Those things make her very angry which coincidentally, usually leads to the very conflict that confirms that she now has that person's attention. As I suggested earlier, this is effective in the short-term if the goal is to get attention. However, if the goal is to find love and nurture and build up a relationship that stands the test of time, it is a very ineffective strategy.

So, Here's What We've Got

When we complete the entire H.E.A.R.T. assessment and put it together in continuous form, it becomes very enlightening. In fact, we actually see how one thing relates to the other and reinforces the entire construct. The original wound or HURT is directly related to the secret hope or EXPECTATION because it's the polar opposite. Then the ASSUMPTION made is a product of the wound which directly lead to the pattern of REACTIONS and TRIGGERS so the whole thing is one giant clusterf*ck of good intentions run amuck. Can you see it?!?

This is what makes it so hard to identify it in the first place. Plus, it also explains why it's so difficult to deconstruct and pull it apart. Every aspect of the wound and response reinforces every other aspect. When you consider that it's been invisibly in place and operating out of sight and out of mind for years and decades, you can start to see why it's so stubbornly resistant and intractable.

While it can be absolutely devastating to your personal relationships due to its ability to remain stealthily out of sight and resist quick and easy healing, let's not forget one very important thing. The entire construct and system is ultimately born of a good and noble intent that came to serve you; it is 100% designed to promote your own healing. Remember: it's a three-part system. We get wounded in relationships. We get triggered in relationships. We get healed in relationships. There literally is no other way or mechanism for us to get back to the truth of who we are and rediscover the unconditional love we want and deserve. But you first have to experience it from within. After all, doesn't it seem kind of irrational to expect perfect, unconditional love from others when you don't love yourself and all your imperfections first? You *are* worthy of love in spite of your imperfections. We *all* are, but it's our responsibility to heal ourselves and *go first.* When you can come to love your own imperfections, it becomes possible to love someone else's. When you harshly judge yourself and withhold love from yourself, you won't be able to drop the judgment and love someone else's imperfection. The fact is, the people who raised you, no matter how awesome and well-meaning, had their own unresolved issues. They were human. It's kind of unrealistic to expect super-human enlightenment from people who were most likely never introduced to their own greatness and humility in equal measure.

- My client, Melinda, was **actually attracted** *to* someone who was <u>emotionally unavailable, lazy, unmotivated and accepted</u>

no responsibility, yet she **actually** *hoped* **he would** be dependable, hard-working and loyal. As a result, her **painful assumption** was that she didn't belong in her own family, she'd never be accepted, and she'd be rejected and abandoned if she ever revealed who she was and how she felt. Understandably, she **learned to react** by giving in, staying quiet for a very long time until she couldn't take it anymore and then she would lash out angrily any time she got **triggered** by feeling dismissed or ignored, ridiculed or yelled at unfairly.

- My client, Sharon, was **actually attracted to** someone who was controlling, bossy, opinionated and critical yet she **actually** *hoped* **he would** be stable, a good listener and fair. As a result, her **painful assumption** was that she had to be perfect, well-behaved and never wrong, otherwise love and approval might be taken away. Understandably, she **learned to react** by retreating into her own world, avoiding confrontations, eating and numbing out by reading or watching TV for an escape. any time she got **triggered** by criticism, name calling or taunting.

- My client, Elaine, was **actually attracted to** someone who had impossible standards, was unpredictable and distant yet she **actually** *hoped* **he would** have high standards, be loyal and hard working. As a result, her **painful assumption** was that she had to become an over-achiever, fulfill other people's expectations rather than her own and never stop working. Understandably, she **learned to react** by withdrawing, hiding in her closet or escaping into a world of make-believe by reading any time she got **triggered** by feeling overwhelmed, over-worked or not good enough.

• My client, Tammy, was **actually attracted to** someone who ignored her, paid no attention to her and had no backbone yet she **actually *hoped* he would** pay attention to her, make her feel loved and important and be strong and unwavering in his support. As a result, her **painful assumption** was that she wasn't enough, no one cared and the only way she could get attention was by creating conflict or getting money, so she uses both as a substitute. Understandably, she **learned to react** by acting out, creating conflict, or medicating her feelings any time she got **triggered** by feeling ignored, unprotected, not getting attention, or seeing weakness.

Are You Ready for the Solution?

Once you use the H.E.A.R.T. Assessment I just shared to create your summary, you'll now have access to the hidden gems that have the power to set you free. That's because those powerful distinctions offer you the new awareness you'll need to start the whole process of healing. It's like seeing the entire game plan laid out in stark, unflinching detail for the very first time with unbelievable clarity. You have now identified the specific hurts and wounds that created the stories that live on in your head and heart, forming the foundation of your doubts, fears and most common modes of self-sabotage. At the same time, you have now articulated exactly why it hurt so much since you've identified what you really secretly hoped to experience instead. By doing that, you can now see the dramatic distance and difference between what you ideally wanted and what you had to settle for due to your powerlessness created in childhood. That, alone, can be a tough pill to swallow since you were an innocent child who deserved better. Once you understand the tremendous gap between your expectations and your experience, you'll see clearly why you made certain assumptions that have not served you or paved the way to love. In fact, these deadly assumptions sabotaged you in having the love you wanted to experience. As a result of this new-found awareness of your stealthy, sabotage patterns, you'll get to come face-to-face with your role in contributing toward any past dysfunction due to your own unresolved issues. Lastly, once you've seen the entire dynamic and how interconnected it really is, you'll now be in a better position to identify any remaining undesired triggers and begin to dismantle them for your highest good.

Okay, so *How,* Exactly, Do We Do That?

With these five simple yet profound revelations, you'll have all the elements you need to begin to reverse the damaging after-effects of your childhood traumas. I have a number of solutions that I will share in this book in order to facilitate your healing which is my ultimate goal for you. By the way, let's be clear here: those old unresolved wounds don't just affect you, they also fail to serve others or the greater good for all. In fact, doing this work I'm about to share with you is a perfect example of a Class III scenario, meaning that it serves you, it serves others and it serves the greater good. One of my key decider strategies in making decisions is whether the outcome is a Class III situation. If it is, then it's an automatic yes from me. I hope you'll consider adopting that standard as well.

Let's begin to flip the script on those unresolved issues that are blocking you from the love you want. They have lingered well into adulthood and have outlived their usefulness. Now that you know about them, it's going to be *so* much harder for you to ignore them. Yeah, that's right. I ruined it for you. Game over. There's no way to un-ring the bell once you've heard it. I promise you, having a real, authentic love when you're healed and whole is so much better than what you've settled for in the past. This is where it starts to get *really* good!

Introducing H.E.A.R.T. Flips™

The first thing I want to share with you is a little device I call H.E.A.R.T. Flips which will help you find an empowered truth. It is literally the exact opposite of all the distinctions you've already identified. We started doing this when we used your Original Wounds to choose your Empathic Expectation, or what you wanted instead. Now we're just going to continue that process on the other 4 aspects of the H.E.A.R.T. Assessment which we previously framed in the negative. While we will address that Empathic Expectation, there's really no need to flip it because it's already framed in the positive. And don't worry if my directions seem confusing at first. I'm going to walk you through a number of examples so it will quickly become obvious and easy. Plus, if you're using my *Companion. Peace.* workbook, you'll be able to simply fill in the blanks on the forms I created just for you.

Hurts - You originally identified three wounds, or dis-appointments, from your childhood and we're going to flip them in order to find a compelling gift or blessing that came directly as a result of that hurt. Remember in each of these four areas, we want it to be a scenario that makes the story serve you, serve others and serve the greater good.

Assumptions - You also identified three assumptions you made based on your beliefs about those wounds and what it meant about you as a child. Now with the clarity of time, wisdom and this new awareness I've given you, we're going to dig back into these stories you told yourself and we're going to harvest a new and improved TRUTH that will serve you instead of debilitating you. The goal here is to help you consciously create what you want by putting you in choice, rather than at effect where you are powerless and at the mercy of whatever happened.

Reactions - You identified three ways your old disempowered reactions sabotaged you due to your lack of understanding based on what you knew at the time. Now that you have a new awareness and a lifetime of adult experience, you will have an opportunity to *consciously choose* how you will *commit* to *responding* instead of unconsciously reacting. This is literally the strategic equivalent of deciding in advance what will work and what you want instead of just settling for what your old triggered responses created.

Triggers - You identified three triggers that, in the past, have brought out the worst in you rather than your best. As I have shared and as you would expect, when you are emotionally triggered by some unresolved wound from your past, you don't respond from a grounded, centered and calm place. You respond from anger, rage, fear or resentment. These are hardly the building blocks of what I like to call a Legendary Love For Life or an effective partnership. (Coincidentally, that's also the name of my relationship coaching business.) I'm going to show you how to consciously choose your response in advance from an empowered state rather than an unconscious reaction from a disempowered state. That kind of flip is literally as profound as night and day.

One More Thing

For those who also ordered my *Companion. Peace.* workbook to accompany this book, the directions below are outlined on the forms provided to conveniently make it even easier to line up the correct answers in the proper place. If you choose to use your own journal or notebook, follow the directions below to get the best results.

- When we fill in the blanks, (1a), (2a) and (3a) are harvested from the three HURTS portion of the H.E.A.R.T. Assessment. The blank lines at (1b), (2b) and (3b) are the flips where you will create new empowering meanings.

- Line (4) is from the Empathic Expectation and it's already framed in the positive so there's no need to flip it. Just copy it here.

- Lines (5a), (6a) and (7a) are harvested from the three ASSUMPTIONS portion of the H.E.A.R.T. Assessment. The blank lines at (5b), (6b) and (7b) are the flips where you will redefine what else those assumptions could mean from an empowered and wiser place.

- Lines (8a), (9a), (10a) are harvested from the three REACTIONS portion of the H.E.A.R.T. Assessment. The blank lines at (8b), (9b), (10b) are the flips where you will now decide and commit to how you will Respond from an empowered place in the future instead of reacting from the old, wounded place.

- Lines (11a), (12a), (13a) are harvested from the three TRIGGERS portion of the H.E.A.R.T. Assessment. The blank lines at (11b), (12b), (13b) are the flips where you will now decide and commit to how you will Respond from an empowered place in the future instead of reacting from the old, wounded place.

Now that we have the answer key out of the way, let's get started. I'm going to walk you through the examples of my clients you've already come to know. I'm going to show you how the new and improved answers fit into my simple and smart format. I think you'll find that this intuitive structure makes rewiring your old beliefs that hold you back a lot easier, more effective and streamlined, too.

Melinda's H.E.A.R.T. Flip:

Although I was an innocent child at the time these beliefs were originally created, here's what I now know for sure in my H.E.A.R.T. and commit to practicing daily:

The truth is, any time I feel like someone is (1a) <u>emotionally unavailable</u>, that simply means that (1b) <u>they're doing the best they can with what they have in the moment</u>. And any time I feel like someone is (2a) <u>lazy and unmotivated</u>, I know for sure that (2b) <u>people's actions are a reflection of their beliefs and experience and that has nothing to do with me</u>.

And when someone is (3a) <u>accepting no responsibility</u>, I just need to remember that (3b) <u>what may bother me the most about that is that I've probably done something similar and I hate when I do it also. So that makes it a perfect mirror for me to examine my own behavior</u>.

Despite all of this, I know beyond shadow of a doubt that I will be healed when I know I was loved, am loved, and am *lovable* just as I am right now.

I also know I have plenty of examples where people were (4) <u>dependable, hard-working and loyal</u> so I definitely know what that looks like and I deserve it!

Even though my assumption was that I (5a) <u>didn't belong in my own family</u>, that is not true because (5b) <u>there have been many examples of where I've been embraced, loved and supported by family members</u>.

And despite my assumption that (6a) <u>I'd never be accepted</u>, the truth is that (6b) <u>feeling accepted by others is simply a reflection of how much I accept *myself*</u>

Lastly, whenever I think about my assumptions like (7a) <u>my fear that I'd be rejected and abandoned</u>, I just need to remember that (7b) <u>while that is perfectly understandable, the problem with assumptions is that they make an ass out of you and me. (ass + u + me)</u>

While I understand why the child in me used to (8a) <u>give in and give up</u>, I now know that the real answer lies in (8b) <u>getting clear on my outcome and asking myself better quality questions about what's really important to me.</u>

Plus, while it's reasonable that a child would feel forced to (9a) <u>stay quiet</u>, I now know that the real answer lies in (9b) <u>speaking my truth from an empowered place and asking for what I want.</u>

And, of course, while a child might predictably (10a) <u>lash out angrily</u>, I know that the real answer lies in (10b) <u>taking back the power I now own as an adult who makes good decisions.</u>

Now whenever I get triggered by (11a) <u>feeling dismissed or ignored</u>, I know that (11b) <u>is a great reminder to me about raising my standards and speaking my truth.</u>

In the future, when I get triggered by (12a) <u>feeling ridiculed</u>, I commit that I will (12b) <u>speak up and demand better or use my power to walk away for good if necessary.</u>

And whenever I feel triggered by (13a) <u>being yelled at unfairly</u>, I can always (13b) <u>take back my power by enforcing a boundary and walking away.</u>

This is my solemn promise and commitment to myself and others. And so, it is.

Do you see how that works now? We simply take this new truth, post it where we will see it daily and recite it out loud as an incantation, utilized to get a new understanding into your body viscerally with power, emotion and spirit. To get it even deeper into your subconscious, move your body as you say it and feel the feelings embedded in these powerful words! Do this every day, as many times as you wish in order to feel great! How long do you think it would take to memorize it, know it by heart and most importantly, LIVE IT?!?

Sharon's H.E.A.R.T. Flip:

Although I was an innocent child at the time these beliefs were originally created, here's what I now know for sure in my H.E.A.R.T. and commit to practicing daily:

The truth is, any time I feel like someone is (1a) controlling and bossy, that simply means that (1b) they have a high need for certainty and order to feel in control and that says far more about them than it ever could about me. And any time I feel like someone is (2a) opinionated, I know for sure that (2b) there's a huge difference between facts and opinions and I now have the right, wisdom and experience to decide what works for me. And when someone is (3a) critical, I just need to remember that (3b) it's my job to define me, no one else's, and if I give that right away for a moment, I can always take it back and keep it for good.

Despite all of this, I know beyond a shadow of a doubt that I will be healed when I know I was loved, am loved, and AM LOVABLE just as I am right now.

I also know I have plenty of examples where people were (4) <u>stable, good listeners and fair</u> so I definitely know what that looks like and I deserve it!

Even though my assumption was that I (5a) <u>had to be perfect to keep love</u>, that is not true because (5b) <u>the truth is we're *all* worthy of love even when we mess up or make a mistake, and that includes *me*</u>!!!

And despite my assumption that (6a) <u>I had to be well-behaved to keep love,</u> the truth is that (6b) <u>I'm a grown-ass woman and now *I get to* make the rules and decide how I will behave because I've earned that right!</u>

Lastly, whenever I think about my assumptions like (7a) <u>I could never be wrong to keep love</u>, I just need to remember that (7b) <u>I've been wrong plenty of times and I'm still loved and worthy of love so that just isn't true!</u>

While I understand why the child in me used to (8a) <u>retreat into her own world</u>, I now know that the real answer lies in (8b) <u>remembering that I'm an adult and if I don't like my world, I have the power to change it as needed.</u>

Plus, while it's reasonable that a child would feel forced to (9a) <u>avoid confrontations</u>, I now know that the real answer lies in (9b) <u>using my ability to influence and negotiate win/win scenarios whenever possible.</u>

And, of course, while a child might predictably (10a) <u>eat and numb out by reading or watching TV for an escape</u>, I know that the real answer lies in (10b) being an active and engaged participant in this life I'm blessed to have!

Now whenever I get triggered by (11a) criticism, I know that (11b) is a great reminder to me about raising my standards and speaking my truth.

In the future, when I get triggered by (12a) name calling, I commit that I will (12b) speak up and demand better or use my power to walk away for good if necessary.

And whenever I feel triggered by (13a) taunting, I can always (13b) take back my power by enforcing a boundary and walking away.

This is my solemn promise and commitment to myself and others. And so, it is.

There's another great example. Different struggles; different solutions. Same process! Post it where you will see it regularly. Turn it into an incantation with power and purpose. Then get it into your body by incorporating movement and passion! You might even want to put a smile on your face and feel it as though it's already a done deal! Learn it; live it; do it!

Elaine's H.E.A.R.T. Flip:

Although I was an innocent child at the time these beliefs were originally created, here's what I now know for sure in my H.E.A.R.T. and commit to practicing daily:

The truth is, any time I feel like someone is (1a) impossible to please with high standards, that simply means that (1b) they're probably just as hard on themselves and it's much more about them and their insecurities than me.

And any time I feel like someone is (2a) unpredictable, I know for sure that (2b) that's probably a signal that I'm trying way too hard to please someone.

And when someone is (3a) critical, I just need to remember that (3b) I don't need to grovel for acceptance anymore because I've decided I'm good enough already and getting better all the time.

Despite all of this, I know beyond a shadow of a doubt that I will be healed when I know I was loved, am loved, and AM LOVABLE just as I am right now.

I also know I have plenty of examples where people were (4) loyal, hardworking and had high standards so I definitely know what that looks like and I deserve it!

Even though my assumption was that I (5a) had to be an over-achiever, that is not true because (5b) if I think about it, there were times when I was less than perfect and they never really did take away their love so I worried for nothing!

And despite my assumption that (6a) I had to fulfill other people's expectations instead of my own, the truth is that (6b) this is my life and the only vote that *really* counts is *mine*!

Lastly, whenever I think about my assumptions like (7a) I could never stop working, I just need to remember that (7b) I am valuable and worthy of love, appreciation and respect just because I'm a child of God!

While I understand why the child in me used to (8a) withdraw, I now know that the real answer lies in (8b) remembering that I made it through, I'm safe, smart and good enough.

Plus, while it's reasonable that a child would feel forced to (9a) hide in her closet, I now know that the real answer lies in (9b) me stepping out in courage and faith.

And, of course, while a child might predictably (10a) escape into a world of make-believe by reading, I know that the real answer lies in (10b) embracing reality and trusting that everything I could ever need to know can be learned if I just. get resourceful enough.

Now whenever I get triggered by (11a) feeling overwhelmed, I know that (11b) no matter how stressed I get, I've always used my experience, work ethic and commitment to figure it out before and I will again.

In the future, when I get triggered by (12a) feeling overworked, I commit that I will (12b) take a deep breath, ask a better question and use the tools I have to manage my state effectively.

And whenever I feel triggered by (13a) feeling not good enough, I can always (13b) choose to love and accept myself right now instead of seeking approval outside of myself since that can be taken away.

This is my solemn promise and commitment to myself and others. And so, it is.

Each one of our examples had unique challenges, beliefs, strengths, weaknesses, opportunities and threats. Some fight while others surrender. Some may find an answer in faith while others may be more agnostic in their approach. The important thing to remember is that this exercise allows you to personalize it in any way that feels right to you. The one thing I can tell you is that if it feels good and makes you smile, that's the right answer.

Then when it feels good, keep doing it over and over and over until it sticks.

Tammy's H.E.A.R.T. Flip:

Although I was an innocent child at the time these beliefs were originally created, here's what I now know for sure in my H.E.A.R.T. and commit to practicing daily:

The truth is, any time I feel like someone is (1a) <u>ignoring me,</u> that simply means that (1b) <u>they have their own needs, desires and interests, too, and when I remember that I am, in fact, enough, people just seem to pay far more attention to me.</u>

And any time I feel like someone is (2a) <u>paying no attention to me,</u> I know for sure that (2b) <u>I can probably get their attention by caring about them first and remembering there are *billions* of people on the planet who care about others.</u>

And when someone is (3a) <u>showing no backbone,</u> I just need to remember that (3b) <u>if I want people to love and accept me as I am, I should probably just drop the judgment and return the favor.</u>

Despite all of this, I know beyond a shadow of a doubt that I will be healed when I know I was loved, am loved, and AM LOVABLE just as I am right now.

I also know I have plenty of examples where people (4) <u>paid attention to me, loved me and supported me</u> so I definitely know what that looks like and I deserve it!

Even though my assumption was that I (5a) <u>wasn't enough and no one cared,</u> that is not true because (5b) <u>they always supported me in their own way even when I was difficult and taught me right from wrong.</u>

And despite my assumption that (6a) <u>conflict equaled attention</u>, the truth is that (6b) <u>I really did cause trouble and antagonize them, so I contributed to it, too.</u> Lastly, whenever I think about my assumptions like (7a) <u>money was an expression of love</u>, I just need to remember that (7b) <u>my parents really did have more money than time so they really *did* do the best they could.</u>

While I understand why the child in me used to (8a) <u>act out</u>, I now know that the real answer lies in (8b) <u>remembering and knowing my own internal value and not begging for scraps of attention from other people</u>.

Plus, while it's reasonable that a child would feel forced to (9a) <u>create conflict</u>, I now know that the real answer lies in (9b) <u>finding better ways to deal with my anger while remembering that conflict and drama isn't love. Love is love.</u>

And, of course, while a child might predictably (10a) <u>learn to medicate her feelings</u>, I know that the real answer lies in (10b) <u>finding appropriate and rewarding ways to express my feelings rather than repress them.</u>

Now whenever I get triggered by (11a) <u>feeling ignored or unprotected</u>, I know that (11b) <u>I can use my own voice and I have the ability to protect myself now.</u>

In the future, when I get triggered by (12a) <u>not getting attention</u>, I commit that I will (12b) <u>use that as a reminder to be more proactive in building new relationships with other like-minded people.</u> And whenever I feel triggered by (13a) <u>seeing weakness</u>, I always (13b) <u>have the strength to choose compassion over contempt.</u>

This is my solemn promise and commitment to myself and others. And so, it is.

There is yet another example of an effective H.E.A.R.T. Flip. Are you getting the idea now? Ready to try your own? The one thing I can tell you for sure is that this is a great tool for forgiving yourself first and then others as well. It's about taking responsibility for whatever shows up not because it's your fault, but because it's your responsibility to clean it up in order for you to live your best life.

Now It's Your Turn

Okay, you know the drill. Before you move on to the next chapter, take the time to do this exercise. This is a very powerful one and it could be the exact thing that cracks it all open and gives you the breakthrough you deserve. Wouldn't that be awesome if you had the most amazing breakthrough ever before you even reached the halfway point?!? I hope you'll give yourself that gift. As I've said before, I really want you to be free and welcome in the kind of joyful and liberating love you deserve. I have purposely stacked these exercises in order, so they tend to build on one another and culminate in some pretty remarkable and powerful epiphanies.

We have a lot more to come and for some, the thing that sets you free will be this exercise we just finished demonstrating. For some, it will come later as we build toward a climax. Still, for others, it might be a valuable distinction from this exercise that when combined with others to come, will be the thing that sets you free and gives you a life and love of your dreams. Whatever it is, you're not going to know unless you stop and *do* this exercise. While you can do the exercise on loose paper, preferably you're doing it in the workbook: *Companion. Peace.* It puts it all together in one place and makes it easy to go through the exercises in one seamless and intuitively-designed experience.

So, get busy. When you're done, I'll meet you in the next Chapter!

Chapter 9:

The ABC's of Healing

 In this chapter, I want to give you some tools to heal any unresolved issues from the past and prepare you to be carried into a brighter, more exciting future. There are a couple of effective ways that will create the kind of movement that will drive you forward. I can stand in front of you and pull you. Or I can get behind you and push you. Either way, you'll move forward.

Think of that force that drives you forward as the power of pleasure. It's the joy you feel when chasing your aspirations. It's the achievement of reaching your dreams. It's the sheer fulfillment of making great things happen. It's the magic that gets you out of bed in the morning and puts a huge smile on your face every time you imagine or consider your goals coming to fruition. Those thoughts can absolutely pull you forward and keep you on track and working hard. While you might think the pursuit of pleasure is a powerful driver, it's really only part of the ultimate achievement equation.

The other part of that equation is ironically its polar opposite. That's because the urge to avoid pain is an even more potent driver than the pursuit of pleasure. Humans will usually run from fear like it's a monster chasing you and that makes fear a powerful force that pushes you from the back. It'll get you running and taking action because you can practically feel it nipping at your heels. But the downside of *only* using fear is that it's draining, eventually exhausting and not sustainable. So, it's only one part of a successful and balanced formula.

For best results, I always suggest combining pleasure *and* pain if you really want to stay committed. In this Chapter, I'm introducing a strategy that harnesses two parts pleasure to one-part pain because I want to help you succeed. By combining both, it's much more positively sustainable without the exhausting side effects of fear only. If you can successfully dance with both pain *and* pleasure, you can learn how to use your emotions instead of letting your emotions use *you.*

This seems like a perfect time to start to introduce my ABC's of Change. The A stands for Aspirations.

Aspirations

Since I just finished writing about the pleasure of achievement or fulfillment, now seems like a good time to consider the idea of your Aspirations. This is where we begin to identify what, specifically, would bring you great pleasure and make you feel proud when it comes to finding love and passion in your life. What kind of relationship do you long to have when you meet your love? How do you want to feel in your relationship? What kinds of things will you celebrate together? Where would you love to go with your partner? What ideas excite you and kind of make your heart race when you think about achieving them together? What's in your heart to achieve before your time on earth is complete? What do you fantasize about sharing with your partner in your mind's eye? Who do you admire or wish you could emulate in terms of their relationship? What legacy of love would you aspire to create? These are just a few of the questions that will help you home in on what would keep you motivated on that path toward your dreams. Oftentimes, your aspirations will be positive and encouraging. But that's not *always* the case.

Closing the Loop

When considering one's aspirations, the idea of closing the loop can be a powerful driver when it comes to goal setting. Think of it as a variation on the Hero's Journey, which is a popular and very common theme used again and again in literature to weave a compelling tale. The story typically follows a broad template of sorts. It generally features a story of a humble protagonist who faces some sort of monumental obstacle that challenges him or her to the core and fundamentally transforms the main character into a hero. Then, once a hero rises to this challenge and conquers it, the compulsion to use that experience and pay it forward is powerful. It's like a chance to leave the world better than you found it. Perhaps you've heard the old saying that the two best days in your life are the day you're born and the day you figure out why. In other words, it's a recognition of the power of how your own self-actualization leads you to finding your calling in life. It's almost like the challenging experience itself was somehow pre-ordained by fate in order to help you discover your purpose or destiny. So, if this is a powerful predictor, what would you say was your "hero's journey" and what did it come to teach you?

For instance, I'm very clear that one of the big reasons I love what I do so much is that as an adopted infant, I didn't always feel the unconditional love I wanted to feel. Let me be clear: that was a painful, recurring feeling that kept replicating across different scenarios including a divorce, multiple breakups and even, most painfully, a period of estrangement from my own daughter. Notice this is exactly the theme of this entire book and it continued for decades until I stumbled upon a learning and means of development that changed all that and helped me heal it. While that's great for me and immensely satisfying to my soul, there's something even more magical when I can help *other people* experience that also. It's almost strange and hard to explain but it is quite a phenomenon. It feels like my whole journey prepared me for the mission I'm on and makes every victory or achievement along the way even more sweet. I want that feeling for you also, and it only comes from doing the work to feel 100% on-purpose and right where you're supposed to be in life.

If you chose this book because relationships have been a place of pain for you, I want to give you some powerful examples of people you may know who transmuted their own personal pain and challenge into great things. Just like I'm demonstrating in this chapter, they also harnessed moving-away energy to avoid pain while harnessing moving-toward energy to pursue the pleasure of their deepest calling. If they can do it, you can absolutely do it also.

These are examples of those who found their calling, and themselves, by pushing against resistance, challenge or even misfortune. At the same time, they listened to the whispers of their soul and an innate knowing that was only satiated by their pursuit of passion.

- Despite an established career on Wall Street, one woman's passion and love for entertaining led her to eventually open a catering firm in Connecticut, then write a book on the Art of Entertaining at the age of 41. That led to a huge global brand you know as Martha Stewart Living.

- After she lost her job as a bilingual secretary for an international human rights group, this British woman lived in absolute poverty. But rather than search for another job, her plan B was to spend time developing an idea she had for a story about the misadventures of a young boy wizard named Harry Potter. It turned out to be a good gamble because it helped J.K. Rowling become the world's first billionaire author solely due to her following her passion for writing and story-telling.

- After a tough stint as a military ambulance driver for soldiers in France during World War I, a struggling commercial artist and cartoonist stumbled onto the art of making paper cut-outs into animated films and cartoons and he became enthralled with it. That artist's name was Walt Disney and it all worked out pretty well for a guy who was once fired from a job because he lacked creativity and original ideas.

Every single one of these individuals turned their challenges into opportunity by simply following their passions, interests and intuition to success. Sometimes, it's not simply a matter of following your passions. Sometimes your biggest tragedy or challenge can help you find your way to your destiny.

Consider these other examples of triumph over extreme adversity:

- Nelson Mandela spent 27 years unjustly imprisoned but instead of embracing hate and revenge, he emerged from prison prepared to lead his country and people toward a new, reunified future.

- Mother Teresa found her calling after coming to India and seeing the crushing need of those who were struggling to simply survive every day. As a result, she founded the Missionaries of Charity, a religious organization dedicated to "wholehearted free service to the poorest of the poor."

- John Walsh's son Adam was brutally murdered in 1981. He eventually channeled his profound grief into a brand-new career as a victim's rights advocate for families and children. He created a non-profit organization in his son's name that eventually merged with the National Center for Missing and Exploited Children. He also inspired changes in Federal and

State legislation. Plus, he served as the TV host on a show called *America's Most Wanted* that specifically resulted in the capture of more than 1,000 fugitives.

While the horrible incidents that preceded these huge and life-changing accomplishments weren't positive or chosen, I simply point out that sometimes enormous, life-affirming blessings that serve the greater good can spring from great tragedy.

Indeed, sometimes only profound tragedy can birth new possibilities due to its ability to cut through our cultural hypnosis, shake us awake and set us on a course toward righting a wrong. In quantum physics, we know that we live in a world of duality where equilibrium and balance must always be maintained. The light always follows the dark and birth will always eventually be followed by death, even if it's unbelievably untimely. The death of an innocent child may be one of the most shockingly painful experiences in the human condition because it feels so unfair and beyond comprehension. It violates all norms and reasonable expectations which is precisely why it cuts so deeply and makes us question everything we thought we knew. People don't necessarily start questioning the meaning of life when an octogenarian dies in their sleep because it follows the "natural order" of things. Of course, we grieve the loss and celebrate their lives, but most people will focus on the fact that they had "a pretty good run." Not so when a child passes unexpectedly.

I'm reminded of an experience I shared with my daughter when she was only 13 years old. As a dad, I always wanted to create teachable moments that would help lay the groundwork for her values and beliefs, and I heard about an event that would help do just that. In March of 2003, in Baltimore, Maryland, a shocking tragedy occurred that left an entire region shaken whether you knew the people involved or not. A beautiful and innocent six-year-old named Annie was leaving the circus with her entire family when a vehicle went out of control, hopped the sidewalk and killed her. In people's grief and mourning, someone was inspired with a vision to create something good out of the despair and tragedy. The vision was to create a safe place for kids to be kids and create the kind of magical memories that last a lifetime. A cause was set in motion. A non-profit foundation was set up and the county where Annie lived donated a large tract of land. Vendors and suppliers donated top-of-the-line equipment and expert services. Businesses and the local government donated labor and machinery for the big jobs. Artists painted murals. Within two years, an army of more than 1,000 volunteers from the community joined forces to work around the clock to open Annie's Playground, the largest, volunteer-built playground east of the Mississippi River in the United States.

The park included some incredible features like a two-story treehouse and jungle gym that I got to help build from the ground up with some of the finest, big-hearted men in my community. It also featured an amphitheater and outdoor classroom, a puppet theater, dragon and elephant slides and a baseball park modeled after our local professional stadium. Then we added a sports complex for recreational sports leagues, walking trails and picnic areas. While I spent days assembling the climbing structure, my daughter donated babysitting services for the other children of volunteers, contributing in a safe and age-appropriate way.

I share this story for a couple of reasons. It was one of the most cathartic and satisfying volunteer experiences of my life (and I love to volunteer and do it fairly often). The reason it was so special is that I shared it with my daughter and some of the most dedicated and big-hearted people I've ever met. The spirit and camaraderie was so powerful and it was a living embodiment for me of the fact that wonderful things can spring from the ashes of unfathomable tragedy. I didn't know Annie, but everyone there felt her unmistakable and beautiful spirit wherever we went. We felt like we were making a difference we could be proud of and creating something special out of our collective grief.

Annie wasn't our daughter, but she was the magical spark that brought us all together. Even though her life was cut far too short, generations of kids, including my own daughter, and my grandson, the child of that same, now-grown daughter, have run around and played on Annie's Playground. Even though the ribbon-cutting was now 15 years ago, their smiles and laughter fill the air and I know that Annie created a great deal of magic in this world in her all-too-brief six years on the planet. If you think about it, some people come into this world and live for decades and decades, but it only took one very special soul about six years to create a lot of magic that will live on forever.

We will all face tragedy and loss in the course of our lifetimes. Sometimes, that tragedy may even introduce you to your life's purpose when you least expect it. My suggestion is always to look for the blessing in every situation and it may be even more critical in the face of tragedy. I believe *everything* comes to serve, even when we don't quite know how. That's when it's most important to look for the empowering meaning.

What Are Your Aspirations of Love?

One of the things that will help give you purpose, vision and commitment is to understand the answer to this foundational question. We're all here for a reason. What's your reason? Take some time and do a little digging here. What is the mission you're here to achieve when it comes to love? If you could only do one thing with your time on earth, what will you leave behind as your legacy of love? Do some journaling or meditation to get some real clarity that feels good to you or puts a smile on your face. Once you get to that smile and feeling of deep satisfaction, trust it and claim it. Even if you have *no* idea what to do to get started, just sit with it. Write it down and start to ask the question, "How can I create even more love right now?" "How can I do/be/have _____?" Trust the process and know that the answer will come in due time when you ask in the exact way I just showed you. The more you think about it, the more clarity you'll find. When you ask great questions, your brain will find a way. When you create doubt and fear by focusing on unproductive thoughts, your brain will confirm what you verbalized by answering terrible questions like, "Who am I to do that anyway?" Questions like that will keep you stuck and struggling. Ask great questions and pay close attention to how you feel. Any time you feel lit up about something, that's a clue for you. Pay attention and claim it. Once you know what the answer is, it's really hard to try to un-ring that bell. Be patient and kind to yourself. It will grow on you and you don't have to know how you're going to do it. It will be revealed soon enough.

After you get some level of clarity on your purpose or aspirations, now we can move to the second phase of the ABC's of Healing.

Benefits

In this phase of the ABC's, we want to continue to stack the benefits in a way that feels good to you and motivates you to do what it takes to stay on track. Again, whatever we link pleasure to has the power to keep us focused in the direction of the dreams we want to create. When you're clear on the benefit of what you want and why, that can be the difference between hitting a snooze button on your alarm or jumping out of bed and taking some kind of clear and productive action in the direction of your dreams. Stacking the benefits will get you to commit to doing an online dating profile instead of just talking about it. It'll get you out of your house, meeting people and enjoying life instead of sitting around waiting for something great to happen when you haven't done anything to *make* things happen. It'll get you to the gym or help you make good, nourishing food choices because you're clear on the importance of your own health.

Stack It High

I'm going to make a bit of an assumption here since you bought a book all about how to understand "Why You Keep Attracting the Same Wrong Partners – and How to Finally Solve It!" It's not going to be a huge stretch either. I'm going to go on the premise that if you picked up this book for two minutes, you may be single and interested in learning more about how to find the love of your life. So, if that's you, I'm going to help you do some of your homework. If that's not you, I'm still going to help you by creating some examples for you to follow. However, they may not apply to you in the same kind of cut-and-paste way that will make your life infinitely easier.

I'm about to create a list of some of the top benefits of WHY you might want to learn to attract the love of your life and how it might make your life presumably better. This is just a partial list. Some of it may apply to you; some may not. Of course, feel free to come up with your own list or add to this list. I wanted to create even more value for you by using a specific example that might inspire you and make you feel good rather than simply describe my stacking process. So, follow along.

The Benefits of Love

1) Every single feature in your 'human highlight reel' will be an act of love.
2) Love is the ultimate guidepost for navigating a life well-lived.
3) Love magnifies the experience of life and enhances it.
4) Love divides the sorrow [or pain] so you don't suffer alone.
5) A loving partner can provide support through challenging times.
6) Experiencing love can make you emotionally healthier.
7) Experiencing love can make you physically healthier.
8) Those who share love tend to live longer, happier lives.
9) A loving relationship can provide emotional intimacy.
10) A loving relationship can provide physical intimacy.

11) A loving relationship can lead to creating a family.

12) Giving love to others is a beautiful game-changer for you.

13) Giving love to others is a beautiful game-changer for them.

14) Demonstrating loving behaviors is a positive influence on your own family.

15) Demonstrating loving behaviors is a positive influence on the world.

16) Having love in your life creates magic moments.

17) Love is the centerpiece for every social celebration.

18) Love is the currency that is exchanged between family and friends.

19) Love creates a community where you can feel at home.

20) Love creates a feeling of safety.

21) Love leads to acceptance and understanding.

22) Love can build a bridge to any destination.

23) Love is your connection to the presence of spirit.

24) When you're connected to spirit, you're connected to love.

25) When you have love, you're never alone.

26) Love and gratitude go together hand-in-hand.

27) Love and happiness increase your odds of finding meaningful work.

28) When you know love, you can know peace. (No love, no peace.)

29) Love is the energy that can attract every good thing to you.

30) Love and passion are closely aligned, so one can lead to the other.

31) The power of love can lead you to your mission.

32) Being in a relationship can multiply your income.

33) Being in a relationship can greatly cut your expenses.

34) Love and money can raise your standard of living.

35) Having love in your life makes you far more resilient.

36) Love literally makes your life about something bigger than just you.

37) Love is a building block for a life of joy.

38) Love is the root of patience and compassion.

39) Love can also give you the leverage to set and enforce healthy boundaries.

40) Acting in love will always keep you on track even when it's hard.

41) Love releases endorphins, dopamine and other pleasure chemicals in your brain.

42) Having love in your heart keeps you youthful and vibrant at any age.

43) Love is the secret ingredient in "regret repellent."

44) A loving smile enhances anyone's looks.

45) When you learn how to love unconditionally, you have mastered life.

46) Acts of love are the basis for all morality.

47) Love is, and always has been, your birthright and your natural state.

48) When you're not sure what to do, ask "what would love do now?" Then do it.

49) Having love in your life makes every single day better. No exceptions.

50) Living with love in your heart is the ultimate success!

Are you starting to see the myriad benefits of love in your life and heart? I just knocked out the first 50 that came to mind because this is what I do: I literally focus on the benefits of love and my gratitude for these magnificent blessings. I did my list. Now it's your turn.

1) What would you add to this list if it was yours?
2) What benefits of love do you see?
3) What benefits do you offer a partner?
4) Why are you committed to having a love of your own?
5) What are you willing to do to have love?

I sometimes give my clients writing exercises to get clear on what they want and why, so I know for sure that some of my clients could knock out a list just as good and send it to me by close of business after a call. I also know that even more of my clients would be struggling to get to five. Whichever group you're in, I hope this list resonates with you and puts a smile on your face. I hope it makes your spirit soar and adds even more love and commitment in your heart. I hope it strengthens your resolve and helps give you the wherewithal to commit to doing what it takes to have love and be love. In short, if this list has helped give you the inspiration to prioritize love, and the will to work to have it, you can absolutely experience this kind of love in your life.

Now just for good measure, let's get to the C in the ABC's of Healing. If you recall, the A was for **Aspirations** and it was specifically designed to get you crystal clear on creating your own "compelling why" when it comes to the reasons you must do the work to create the kind of love you deserve. (Yes, you really do. I heard that self-doubt.) The B was for **Benefits** and it was designed to stack all the blessings that were and are available to you and get you excited and inspired for what you can have if you really want it. I hope that list still has you smiling in anticipation of all the gifts that are really yours for the taking. Lastly, let's get to the C, because that's designed to put the finishing touch on this little triumvirate of triumph.

Costs

C is the one-part pain that creates leverage. It's designed to get you clear on the **Costs** of *not* doing what needs to be done in order to have what you want. In other words, if you don't dig in and do the work, it will potentially cost you every single thing you may have been excited about wanting.

I want to get really clear on why doing the work I'm about to share is a MUST. I want you to have the leverage you're going to need to push through when things get tough. I want to make sure you don't just quit on yourself, or me, and give up if you run into a little discomfort or even pain.

This can be challenging; I'm not going to lie. You may not like revisiting that which makes you uncomfortable and I totally get that. We're going to take a look into the shadows where you may not like to look, and some of it may not feel good. However, I promise you this, those shadows get distorted by perspective. For example, when you stand on the street early or late in the day and it looks like your shadow is 30 feet tall when you're not even six feet tall. That is the gross distortion I want you to recognize.

Don't believe everything you think. Even though something might seem bigger, darker and scarier in the moment, it is *not*. You are still you, a multi-dimensional being with unique thoughts, ideas, experiences and nuances. Some of those things may have caused pain, some may have created joy, and some have led to a mixture of both.

In the coming pages, you will see how all of it served you, even the stuff you didn't like or want. You are not that distorted, dark shadow that appears ominous at first glance. You are a glorious and complex soul who will never be reduced to a simple absence of light, no matter how much it resembles you or doesn't. If you made it through this far, you are safe. You are okay and you will be just fine.

You're already on the absolute right track just by reading this book. By being here and choosing to read this far, you have already shown and proven that you are stronger and tougher than your old fears or sad stories. Even if you've been abused outrageously and unfairly, thinking about it is not the same as being victimized by it again. There will be no new scars or bruises. You are safe and we are in the progress of making sure you can't be harmed that way ever again. Of course, you're free to stop reading at any point and if you feel triggered beyond your comfort zone in reading this, I invite you to reach out to me in person at <u>dave@legendaryloveforlife.com</u>.

Let's Get Some Clarity

If you're ready to begin this leverage exercise, I want you to consider the following questions and write your answers in either a notebook or in the *Companion. Peace.* workbook that goes with this book. Feel free to write in a stream of consciousness or in the form of one continuous rant. Or you can answer the specific questions one at a time and in depth. Do whatever you need to do to get the result. I want you to *feel* some of the emotional intensity of this, but you will not *stay* here. I want it to be brief but effective so that you get the desired result. I am specifically challenging you to give yourself a limited and measured dose of pain in order to create a catharsis of clarity of why change is a must and why it must happen now.

It's been said that everything great, valuable and life-changing will occur just outside your comfort zone. So now is the time to get a little uncomfortable. Just like a vaccination is a minute dose of a toxin designed to let your immune system create antibodies to heal a disease and prevent it from spreading, I want you to use a disassociated memory of your past experiences to create the leverage or wherewithal to never let that pain harm you again. A disassociated memory is an awareness of a situation from a distance. So rather than recalling a painful experience by reliving it as if it is happening to you, again, you will imagine the experience while you watch it happening on a movie screen. The most important part is that you change the perspective from happening *to you* to happening *to someone who looks like you* but from a safe distance. You can always reduce the pain or fear by imagining the scene darker, or farther away, or without sound. Basically, you now have the power to RE-present the situation in a way that makes it more manageable.

If it is too painful to relive in the way I've described, you can also do what's known as a double disassociation. That would be you imagining yourself in the projection room of a movie theater looking down upon yourself, sitting in the audience, watching the screen so you are two stages removed from what's happening and perfectly safe. The key is to use what happened to you to empower yourself to create all new possibilities instead of disempowering you as you presumably may have done in the past. I literally want you to be able to "flip the script" on what happened to you so that you can reveal and heal rather than conceal and not feel.

I'm now going to ask you a number of questions designed to give you a powerful and compelling reason as to why you literally have no choice but to change and change now. These questions are somewhat tough and are purposely meant to be confronting and uncomfortable. I don't do it to cause you pain. I do it to jar your subconscious conditioning and give you clarity. I never want to purposely cause you pain or hurt you in any way, but I also want to be clear that you are not fragile or broken. You cannot resolve that which you refuse to observe or acknowledge. This is no time for softeners and niceties. That is why you might be stuck in a situation that is far less than what you truly deserve. By pushing you outside your comfort zone, and accompanying you on that journey, I simply want to support you and help you be free.

Buried pain is like a prison sentence with no chance of parole, and I care about you too much to just keep you locked up with no end in sight. So, please, let's do this. Don't just read it either. Write it down so you get clarity. It's perfectly okay if you cry or get emotional during this process. It's far better to get that out and release it than to keep it bottled up inside anyway. You'll be okay. That kind of trapped energy is absolutely toxic, and it causes disease in the body. Push yourself and feel some of that pain that you probably keep pushing down to avoid it. I promise, if you'll feel it for a relatively brief time period, freedom and joy await on the other side when you get the answers you need. So, let's get started:

1) What's going to happen if you don't address this now?
2) What's it going to cost you?
3) What will you never get to experience?
4) Where will you never get to go or enjoy?
5) Who won't be in your life anymore?
6) Who will never show up because of this?
7) Who might get disgusted or frustrated and just give up on you?
8) What will that do to your health?
9) How miserable will you be if this doesn't change?
10) What do you think this problem is doing to your finances?
11) How might this affect your faith or spirituality?
12) What's going to happen to you if you can't find faith or believe in something?
13) Who might leave your family if you don't solve this?
14) Who's going to start avoiding you, or just stop coming around?
15) How is this affecting your career?
16) What job are you going to be stuck in because of this?
17) What job or opportunity are you never going to get?
18) What will your colleagues think about you?
19) What will your boss think about you?
20) What's going to happen if you keep settling?
21) What's life going to look like if you never speak up or tell the truth?
22) If we don't change this *now*, how much worse will it be a year from now?

23) How about two years from now if nothing changes?

24) What if it goes five more years without a change?

25) Where will your health be then?

26) Who will have just had it by then and walked away?

27) How about your finances after five more years of this?

28) What kind of shape do you think you'll be in a decade from now?

29) Imagine another 10 years of this. Are you okay with that?

30) How do you think you're going to age with this kind of stress?

31) Imagine 10 more years of this strain on your health. Will anyone be there to take care of you?

32) Imagine how tired and worn out you'll be after 10 more years of this crap. What is that like?

33) How about 15 more years of this?

34) What about 20 years from now, what chance will be gone forever by then?

35) Now stack on another five years of regret, 25 years of wasted chances. What is that like?

36) How are you going to live with the fact that you didn't even try?

37) What's going to happen when your window of opportunity closes for good?

38) How will it feel to know that opportunity knocked and you didn't answer?

39) What are you doing to when it's too late to live your dream?

40) How are you going to explain to people why you never took a shot on love?

41) How will you live with the guilt of your poor decisions?

42) What kind of shame are you going to feel if you don't take action now?

43) What are you going to regret 30 years from now if you don't just do it?

44) Who will you never get to meet because of your fear?

45) What is your lack of faith going to cost you that you'll never experience?

46) What will your life be like 40 years from now? 50? 80?

47) How much longer are you going to play small and settle for mediocrity?

48) What regrets are you going to take to your grave?

49) What are people going to say about you when you're gone?

50) What would it feel like to meet the person you could have been?

Sorry About That

Okay, I apologize if that stirred up some pain. I promise you, though, there is a reason why I asked you do that. First, I want you to know that you are not brittle or weak. If you're reading this, you made it through the tough part and you're still here. So, acknowledge yourself and your own innate toughness. Well done! Second, I want you to be really clear on why these old fears, stories and insecurities MUST change now. You deserve to be free and you can't, or won't, get there if you're not 100% committed to taking action and doing what is necessary to get the result. The choice is and has always been yours.

Ironically, just today I got a client right to the root of her struggles. However, despite showing her how to reopen the lines of communication with a man she loved even after she totally sabotaged everything, she has opted not to continue coaching. Basically, she reached places she didn't want to go and while she was grateful for my help, she decided she did not want to continue. I've never had that happen before, but I found out along the way that the woman is haunted by the brutal murder of a family member years ago and has internalized her post-traumatic stress into intractable fear and trust issues that she doesn't want to explore or heal. It's absolutely not her fault that her cousin was murdered by her husband and now she can't trust men, but she is paying a tragically high cost for that trauma. It makes me sad for her because I really liked her and wanted to see her be free. But I can't make her do the work. I laid it all out for her. I showed her both specific examples of how she was being held back, and I also shared the way forward. We were so close. Ultimately, I have no choice but to accept her decision.

The sad thing is that I predict and fully expect that the relationship hanging by a thread will probably be irreparably broken by the end of the weekend. She's had it happen before and I made her aware of it. I share this story, because it is a timely and perfect reminder of why a simple lack of resolve, willingness or motivation will block your best efforts every time. It doesn't matter what people say they want. This lady was all-in on finally cleaning up her relationship mistakes and repairing things with her ex-boyfriend when she thought it was a communication issue. However, when she discovered how and why she was struggling due to a traumatic event that occurred in her family more than two decades ago, she wasn't prepared for that and ran the other way. In the meantime, I send her my very best and hope that one day, when she's ready, I'll hear from her again. This story is a cautionary tale about why it's so very important to clearly and viscerally want to heal and resolve any lingering issues. Also, the timing of this happening as I was writing the chapter is no accident. I want you to see and feel what it's like for an innocent person to choose to stay stuck despite your own good wishes on their behalf. But there's one more important reason I shared it: it's always easier to see "your own stuff" in the actions of someone else.

That's *why* I pushed you in this Chapter and had you confront some painful things. I wanted you to convert that pain into the necessary fuel you're going to need to do the work. I want you to be clear on the cost of giving up, losing interest or quitting because it's too easy to do, especially when things start to get tough. There's something powerfully motivating about the need to avoid further pain and that's why we use it. In fact, it's probably twice as strong as its transverse quality, the pursuit of pleasure. Think about it: from an emotional standpoint, you'd probably do more to avoid having someone steal $20 from you than you would ever do to invest or save $20. The pursuit of pleasure just doesn't motivate you in quite the same way as the fear of loss. So, if you can torture yourself by worrying about things that'll never ever happen for no good reason, I'm sure you'll understand why I wanted to use it constructively to help you. Sometimes a metaphorical dog nipping at your heels will help you reach the speed you need to be safe and free. So, keep running! We've got this.

History shows that leverage works to create the kind of long-lasting and permanent change you deserve. When you start with linking an action or inaction that is sabotaging you to massive pain and then create a constructed, abject fear of future consequences, it is a powerful driver of change.

Let's be clear: you have a real chance to change right now, right here, in real time. I hope you got that and took advantage of it by using that opportunity to feel the pain of failure you will experience if you *don't* change. Simply put, champions aren't created by choosing ease, comfort and mediocrity over excellence. As Muhammed Ali once said, *"I hated every minute of training, but I said, 'Don't quit. Suffer now and live the rest of your life as a champion."*

Chapter 10:

Same Old Story – Brand New Happy Ending

Now that we've gotten clarity on our past, present and future, we should have the leverage to keep you accountable for taking the necessary action to get traction on your new goals. In Chapter 9, we took some time to learn our ABC's when it comes to that which you want more than anything else. We identified our **Aspirations** in order to keep us moving forward in the direction of our goals. We got crystal clear on all the myriad **Benefits** that will surely follow as long as you set a new standard and stay committed to these new possibilities. After we got two parts pleasure in the form of aspirations and benefits, we added one-part pain just to keep you balanced and honest as you're moving forward and solidifying some new empowering actions and habits. That's why we got clear on the **Costs** and what you'd miss out on if you don't stay on track. Hopefully, that kind of clarity will keep you making progress, which is simply another word for happiness. As long as you're growing, you can feel good. The problems begin when we stop growing or become stagnant.

If you didn't do the work in the two previous Chapters, you really owe it to yourself to stop, go back and do it. If you don't have some pages of notes, a newfound commitment and a desire to have what you deserve, you may not have the resolve to push through resistance and stay on track when life happens and you get distracted, tired or even discouraged. The best tip I can give you to keep making progress is to write your goals in a compelling way that makes you feel good and revisit them often, so they stay top-of-mind as you go about your life making decisions. I've seen that formula work for me and so many others, so I'm confident that it can work for you also. Everything you want is just ahead, outside of your comfort zone, so let's keep going.

We're going to start to do some heavy lifting, also known as healing. We're going to get clear on any lingering or unresolved wounds so that we can clean them up and bring some resolution. In order to do that, I'm going to help you identify them first so we can see if these often seemingly forgotten incidents may still be holding you back in some way. Then once we identify them, we will re-interpret and equilibrate any strong emotions that may be sabotaging you, whether it's happening silently or right out in the open.

If you're not clear on what that means, let me give an example. For some people with unresolved wounds from relationships, they will put up huge walls around themselves with the positive intent to keep themselves "safe." They may avoid relationships or intimacy, claiming no interest in or time for such things. They may even have a good or even tragic story why that's the case. We probably all know someone who's done that or is doing that right now. In fact, some of you who are reading this may be doing it at this very moment. It is a great example of someone whose unresolved wounds linger openly.

At the same time, there is another group of people who don't have an aversion to relationships at all. They may even pursue them openly and seemingly welcome the intimacy that's part and parcel of the typical romance. But all is not what it appears at times. The people in this group try to keep their wounds hidden, even from themselves. They'll get into relationships, but they'll also get out of them quickly when their unresolved "stuff" triggers them, occasionally without warning. They'll walk because of unfair expectations or angry reactions triggered by buried wounds. They may even run the other way when there's a perfectly good explanation for a behavior that remotely resembles an old wound. They may end a relationship because someone didn't call when they expected they would or if a partner travels for work more than they think they should. These triggers may seem hidden, if you don't know what you're looking for, but I'd say it was right there hiding in plain sight the whole time. The story seems plausible, so they don't do any inquiry about *why* they feel that way, and that just means they'll experience it again in another form.

I am committed to changing that for you. Even though it may seem like it could be painful to clean the infection out of an open wound, just leaving it in there is an even worse solution. If you don't clear out that which prevents your healing, there really is no way to heal. If you try to ignore it, that doesn't mean it will go away. On the contrary, it only gets worse and worse, not to mention more stubborn and difficult to heal. I sincerely hope you'll take this opportunity to do this healing work now, and I would be honored if you allow me to be your guide. I've helped a lot of people through this process and I've watched miracles occur. I've seen people heal estranged relationships with their parents or other family members. I've seen clients make peace with departed family members. I've seen people rescind divorce papers already filed. Plus, I've watched so many clients attract Legendary Loves that culminate in engagements, marriages and babies. I tell you all this to confirm and promise you that healing *is* not only possible, but almost unavoidable if you just do the work. So please join me and let's keep going. Together. We've got this.

Cleaning Up the Past

The work always begins with identifying that which needs healing and shining a light on it. You may have heard it said that light is a great disinfectant and it's absolutely true. As you illuminate old, forgotten wounds, you'll shed light on the new possibilities ahead, leaving old hurts behind. As we redefine those old wounds with all-new eyes, we leave behind the pain and insecurity created when they were first introduced. Many of those wounds happened in your childhood when you had no chance to prevent or mitigate them. You were young, inexperienced and had no power. You had little experience or wisdom when it came to the ways of the world. You literally had no chance to defend the indefensible. Nor could you even properly put things in

161

perspective in your own mind in a way that didn't cause you pain or confusion.

Today, however, is a new day. You picked up this book and have already read it this far. You're still here and that tells me there's something special in you and you won't be denied. You pushed through when things got tough. You did the work and kept going. The good news is that this is the point where things are going to start getting good. This is where the true healing starts because we are going to re-define things in a way that feels a whole lot better than anything you've been lugging along thus far. This is where we put down the baggage, let go of pain, resolve old hurts for good. You don't have to carry that stuff around anymore. It's exhausting! You don't need it. Once you get the lesson, you can drop it for good.

Everything Comes to Serve

This can be a difficult concept to wrap your head around but once you manage to do it, freedom awaits on the other side. We already talked about how tragedy can serve and even how bad things can lead to good outcomes. When you start to let go of characterizing things as good or bad, and instead see them as simply contrast between two possibilities, you're almost there. For instance, sometimes we have to experience what we absolutely *don't want* in order to discover what we *do want*. Sometimes we need to get challenged like we've never been challenged before to actually see what we're made of and what we're committed to having or doing in life. Occasionally, it's the loss that we desperately don't want that provides the fuel and inspiration to accomplish great things. The fact is, all human achievement usually comes from pushing *against* something, or being pushed *by* something.

Now, we are going to pay special attention to the unresolved R.O.O.T. issues from childhood that we discussed earlier in the book. If you recall, I defined a R.O.O.T. issue as your Relationship Origin of Trauma. Every one of these traumas is created by certain unique human behavioral patterns. Let's be clear that we are going to talk about a wide range of behaviors here. Some may be more innocent than others like the proper and well-intended correction of a child's inappropriate behavior by a parent. While it is the job of a parent to teach socially acceptable behavior to their children, if it is internalized as shameful by the child, there may be some perceived "trauma" from the child's perspective even if it is wholly unintended or possibly even unwarranted. Remember, we're talking about the impressions of a child at their level of understanding and experience. Let's be clear: there is a world of difference between correcting a child and abusing one and I am in no way conflating the two. If this book helps create even one more awakened parent who is conscious of the huge distinction between criticizing a child's behavior, instead of the child, or one more adult who finally heals age-old beliefs about their own self-worth due to parental actions or inactions, I will consider this book a phenomenal success. The great news is that I see that happening every day in my coaching and in speaking appearances, so I am confident that is already occurring.

On the opposite end of that spectrum of behavior would be outrageous acts of physical, mental, emotional or sexual abuse or neglect. None of these acts are appropriate, fair or even defensible and there is no acceptable explanation or rationale for the infliction of this kind of (mis)behavior on any child.

That being said, these abuses have been part of the human experience since the beginning of time. Sad to say, they will, unfortunately remain a part of the human experience because people who've been hurt will often hurt others in very similar ways. Accepting this fact should not be mistaken for condoning the behaviors. We do not condone it in any way, shape or form. However, if we can unite with a realistic goal of drastically cutting the prevalence of these types of incidents, limit the damage and actually **heal** those affected, which is the specific purpose of this book, we can literally create a world of difference. If we can heal people so they *don't* act out their own abuse, we can make massive progress toward ending this kind of injustice in every successive generation.

In quantum physics, there is an understanding that what is repressed in the masses is expressed in the individuals. It's like grabbing a handful of sand at the beach. The harder you squeeze it, the more will be squeezed through your fingers. The unavoidable reality is that as long as individuals can meet their needs as they perceive them in the moment through acts of abuse, we will have abusers walking amongst us. I don't write that to scare you. I write it to educate you. Of course, we crack down on offenders when identified but that's just one aspect of the solution if we seriously want to change this and make a difference. We need to rethink our objectives and come up with a holistic, all-encompassing approach that helps to enlighten the public about what to look for to prevent acts of abuse.

In addition, we also have to remove the stigma of shame while supporting victims with treatment. Since child abuse is simultaneously one of our society's greatest taboos and fears, you could rightly make the case that it begets a great deal of concern and worry. While that is a good and noble intent to protect our society's most vulnerable, we should beware that the unintended consequence of that collective belief is that our own worst fears could exacerbate the damage we most want to avoid. As someone who works on the front lines of healing abuse, human beings can be remarkably resilient. If they believe they are a victim of an unforgivable sin that forever stains and defines them, their freedom becomes unlikely and they become their own jailer holding the key. I do not subscribe to that belief and I hope you won't either. If they, like me, believe they can be healed, miracles are possible. I have an unlimited amount of compassion but precious little pity because pity only keeps people stuck and serves no one.

Too often, this kind of abuse is unreported and unpunished, and one reason is due to the stigma of shame that silences those who might otherwise speak up and find their voice. Sure, occasionally there are very serious punishments meted out, but even in the best of circumstances we have to realize that there are many more offenders going unpunished than the ones who are caught and prosecuted. Abuse happens in the dark, behind closed doors. So, our best approach is to bring the light and its disinfecting powers. Ironically, abuse is often aided and abetted by the emotional effects of abuse. It's literally, the shame, itself, that keeps victims suffering and prevents those in the know, like family members, from reporting it. This is untenable if we really want to do something about the problem. The innocent victims should not be the ones suffering in silence. They shouldn't be the ones feeling all alone and unsupported. They shouldn't have to carry a burden of shame they did nothing to deserve or warrant. They shouldn't be threatened or beaten into compliance and silence. They shouldn't have to live in fear, pain or dread of future abuse to follow.

If I sound passionate about this topic, it's because I am driven by my COMpassion. I've heard too many stories from too many people and I've seen the weight they carry unnecessarily. If it's the compassion that drives me to write this book and make a difference, it's the effect I get to see and celebrate when I witness clients *freed* from that which once imprisoned them that makes me passionate. I've seen them rediscover joy and confidence. I've seen them embrace their stories and rise above them, never to be haunted by them ever again. I've seen them find love and celebrated their weddings with them. I've watched babies born to new, healthier couples. I literally walked them through the valley of their deepest pain, and I walked them out to the other side where joy and freedom awaited! *That* is what lights me up and *that* is why I wrote this book. So, if you're ready to be accompanied by a very seasoned guide and protector as we briskly walk through your own personal valley of pain to emerge on the other side where joy, passion, forgiveness and all good things await, take my hand and let's do this!

As We Begin This Journey Together

I want to know what you're taking with you. I'm speaking

specifically about your beliefs and expectations because let's be clear: mindset matters. We're about to make some big changes and like any productive, rewarding journey, it starts with being clear on your destination, knowing exactly what you need and leaving behind that which you don't. I suggest we take an open mind, a positive attitude and a belief that good things are possible for those who do the work. Are you willing to do that? And while we're preparing for the journey, I suggest we leave behind any old ideas that no longer serve you like thinking of yourself as some kind of a victim. Labeling yourself as a "victim," by definition, gives your power and agency over to someone else you label as the "abuser." While I'm not excusing anyone's bad behavior or withholding compassion from someone who was wronged and deserves it, I'm just pointing out that the unintended consequence of entering that victim/abuser power dynamic on either side doesn't bode well if you want to escape it.

You're reading this book to find out how you can change and heal unresolved wounds. You can't do that unless you're willing to discard that "victim" label. So, do us both a favor and visualize you peeling off a bright yellow label on your shirt that says "victim," and crumple it up so the adhesive sticks it together and can no longer be pulled apart without tearing. Once you do that, you can no longer re-apply that label, so the only thing you can do is crumple it completely into a tight, sticky ball and throw that useless clump it in the garbage where it belongs. Just doing that little visualization is kind of cathartic, especially when you start to add feelings like pride, toughness, and blessed to the mix. Notice that every sticky label we apply has an emotional charge that comes with it that permeates everything about the wearer of that label.

In fact, let's do a comparison so you get this. Visualize two people standing in front of you with big yellow labels on their shirts. One label says "victim." The other says "survivor." Look at how the victim is standing. Is their posture tall and proud or weak and slumped? Do they speak with assurance and confidence or are they tentative in their speech and unsure of every word? Do they focus on being *blessed* or *oppressed*? Are they excited about life and the possibilities ahead or are they intimidated and overwhelmed by pretty much anything? Now look at the person wearing the "survivor" label, or even better, imagine their label says "thriver." Notice how that person stands. Notice how they think and speak with assurance. Think about what they believe and how they approach life. Do you think a thriver is going to be more empowered and bolder than someone with a victim identity? Of course, they are, because words have meaning, and meanings create emotion. So, let's be clear and make sure that if anything sticks with you it's this: whatever follows the words "I AM" follows you. I am a survivor. I am a thriver.

You picked up this book because you want change. You want love. You want hope. You want joy. I can take you to those things, but this is where we decide. If you come with me, your old victim label stays behind. It is useless to you and will no longer serve a purpose. It will only keep you stuck if it's stuck on you. So, if you're ready to lose that label for good and move forward to find the love, hope and joy you deserve to feel, let's get busy.

I'm going to push you. I don't want to see you left behind with old labels of victimhood stuck on you. However, I'm also clear that it's not my choice. It's yours. If you're ready for freedom, a standard of living and a life that no "victim" will ever know, just tell yourself that you're ready and let's do this. If you get triggered by anything in this chapter, you should know that it's the old victim mentalities getting stirred up again. So be vigilant and be ready. Just remind yourself that you made a choice to give yourself this gift. So, let's read on and say goodbye to victimhood. We've got this.

The 12 Traumatic M.I.S.B.E.H.A.V.I.O.R.S.™

As you can see, I like using acronyms to unpack a large amount of related information. I find it helps me to remember it as I'm teaching it, plus it helps the people who are learning it to recall it. That's why I've created a list I call the 12 Traumatic M.I.S.B.E.H.A.V.I.O.R.S.™ that are directly and most often responsible for these wounds that linger deep in the receiver's subconscious well into adulthood. You can pretty much think of these (mis)behaviors as "the dirty dozen" when it comes to outrageous acts of abuse inflicted on innocent and practically defenseless children. Perhaps worst of all, these acts aren't usually perpetrated by shadowy strangers with ill intent. They're usually inflicted by trusted adults including the parents, caretakers, family members or other adult authority figures who are in proximity to or well-known to the child who is victimized. In this case, the "child" we're talking about is probably you.

Some of you may not like these behaviors described as "trauma-inducing" because it may make it sound worse than you want it to sound. While I never want to make anything worse than

169

it is, I also want to be clear that you are not over-reacting in any way if some of these misbehaviors have left you with sensitivities, insecurities, fear or even harm many years later. In fact, it's these *actions* that have directly led to the less-than-helpful thoughts beliefs and behaviors that have the power to haunt you years and decades later. I'd much rather acknowledge them as legitimate than pretend they didn't exist, because that is *literally* the path to taking back your power. So, feel what you feel and own it, because no one else gets to define you. That's your job and yours alone.

As we're going through this list and seeking a new understanding that can free you, you may have a tendency to distance yourself, deny some deep feelings or feel a compulsion to make allowances for the people who've hurt you, especially if the adult is a parent. I promise you, those inclinations will not help you at all and will only keep you stuck. I have no intention of inflicting unnecessary pain on you. Likewise, it is not at all my intent to create dissension and anger between you and any implicated family members. It is not a betrayal or wrong to identify and acknowledge that which hurt you. We're not going to keep you stuck and angry here. That wouldn't be productive at all. My goal is to glean the necessary lessons and gifts from your experiences while embodying the compassion and forgiveness that can set you free. So, with that in mind, let's identify the 12 Traumatic M.I.S.B.E.H.A.V.I.O.R.S. that may have caused you harm and as we acknowledge them, remember we are simultaneously beginning to heal them. Once we cover the behaviors briefly, we are going to unpack the benefits and believe it or not, the ways they actually *served you.*

The 12 Traumatic M.I.S.B.E.H.A.V.I.O.R.S.

Manipulation
Injustice
Shame
Betrayal
Exploitation
Humiliation
Abandonment
Violence
Isolation
Objectification
Rejection
Sexual assault

Let's go into a little more detail on the 12 M.I.S.B.E.H.A.V.I.O.R.S. that may have created some wounds for you.

1) Manipulation

Manipulation is defined as an attempt to control or play upon another person by using artful, unfair, or insidious means. It's when someone strategically tries to take advantage of you by what they may say or do, or not say or do, for that matter. Some common ways this happens is when someone specifically seeks to make you feel guilty about something or not good enough in some way. Another way this occurs is through a technique called gaslighting. It's when someone specifically attempts to make you doubt your own memory, perception or sanity by constantly challenging your own impressions until you no longer trust your own senses.

The Effect: In the short-term, this might cause confusion, uncertainty and a definite lack of confidence. Over time, as these effects stack and accumulate, they can result in hopelessness, surrender and even an incapability to attempt anything.

The Goal: In order to heal this, it's our job to rediscover your autonomy and will, and find your own voice once again.

The Gift: Now this is important: the gift is always in the turnaround. The gift of having been manipulated by others *in the past* is that once you become aware, as you are now, you become forced to develop your own strength of internal knowing. *You* literally become the voice in your head instead of giving that awesome power away to others who don't deserve it and haven't earned it. You actually learn to trust yourself. That is a precious gift that will serve you well forever as you become internally directed by your own thoughts and feelings rather than externally motivated by other people's thoughts, words or beliefs. Only someone who has been robbed of the ability to be their own internal voice can truly know how precious that ability is, how easily it can be lost and how important it is to maintain. Those who've had that experience become exceptional at guarding it in the future once they get it back and they will never let it go again. It's

172

like that old saying "you don't know what you've got until it's gone," and once you do the work to get it back, you won't make that mistake again.

2) Injustice

This occurs when a party is treated unfairly or when their rights are violated, especially with a willful disregard. This also covers inhumane treatment where a party's inherent worth is ignored or overlooked.

The Effect: In the short term, victims may attempt to resist or fight back but those who are treated unjustly over long periods of time give up their own autonomy and settle into feelings of helplessness and hopelessness.

The Goal: Regain the ability to stand your ground, speak your truth, take back your own power and reconnect to a sense of right and wrong.

The Gift: The gift of having been unjustly treated by others *in the past* is that once you become aware, as you are now, you become forced to develop your own internal sense of right and wrong. You get crystal clear on your own values, beliefs and ideals that drive you so you never give them away again. It is absolutely life-changing to have such a powerful, internal compass pointing the way forward. It becomes highly unlikely that you'll ever get high-jacked again by less-principled individuals than you. When you have that level of newfound clarity on who you are, what drives you and why, it gives you a super power that can focus you in the direction of your dreams, goals and aspirations in a way that is powerfully game-changing.

3) Shame

This painful emotion is caused when another person seeks to instill a consciousness of guilt, shortcoming, or impropriety on another. Brene Brown, a noted researcher on the topic of shame, defines it as a feeling of being flawed and therefore unworthy of love and belonging due to something we've experienced, done, or failed to do that makes us unworthy of connection.

The Effect: Brown also opines that shame can lead to destructive, hurtful behavior and is seldom productive. She also believes that the fear of disconnection can make us dangerous because it pushes us toward a greater desire for self-preservation. She points out that those who feel isolation, disconnection and loneliness try to protect themselves, leading to less empathy, more defensiveness, more numbing, and less sleeping.

The Goal: In order to restore a healthy self-image, it requires you to reject the opinion of those who seek to shame you and restore your own ability to decide what is shameful and what is not.

The Gift: The gift of having been shamed by others *in the past* is that once you become aware, as you are now, you become forced to shrug off the beliefs and perceptions of others who seek to limit you due to their *own* fears, insecurities and disabling beliefs. *You* literally *decide* that while you have no need to be perfect, since that's an illusion anyway, you are going to learn to focus on the things you *do* like about you instead of that which causes you to feel less than confident. There is an awesome power available to those who grapple with the devil of shame and insecurity, only to discover that you actually like yourself just the way you are and even embrace your own vulnerability and imperfection. You learn that real strength isn't about doing what everyone else in the world seemingly agrees that you should do in any given situation. Real strength is vulnerably deciding what you're going to do in advance. You start to develop trust in *you* rather than in your ability to maintain the good opinions of others.

4) Betrayal

This occurs when someone you'd like to think has your best interests in mind takes complete advantage of your trust or confidence by putting their own needs or the needs someone else ahead of yours. It can also occur when someone falls far short of an expected moral standard.

The Effect: It can be absolutely crushing when you discover that you've been used and abused when you least expected it in spite of your perceived connection with another person or people. While you may assume someone has a duty of care and wouldn't purposely hurt you, occasionally other people's agenda gets revealed painfully and publicly. It can be nearly impossible to trust again.

The Goal: Once your trust has been violated so egregiously, it's important that you learn to trust again while doing it far more intelligently. You'll also need to develop your own intuition and abilities to do proper due diligence in relationships.

The Gift: The gift of having been betrayed by others *in the past* is that once you become aware, you learn to go internal and trust *yourself* instead of seeking to trust others who may have competing or misaligned interests, desires or goals. While it's painful when people you trust let you down, especially when you're a child, the real benefit comes when you start to realize that most people do make decisions in their own perceived best interests, and that has nothing to do with you. Of course, it's an outrage when someone takes advantage of a child's innocence, but that very violation becomes the gift that teaches people how to trust *themselves*. It teaches courage, resilience, faith and it absolutely develops skills and abilities that will change your life for the better, forever.

5) Exploitation

This is what happens when someone uses their power, influence or your trust to take advantage of you or harm you in some way for their own personal benefit. It's indefensible and wrong on every level.

The Effect: Those who've been exploited by others can develop life-long trust or possibly shame issues that can manifest in a number of ways. Some put up walls, keep people at a distance and retreat within. Some scrutinize people unfairly and look for what's wrong constantly which can result in feelings of isolation and loneliness.

The Goal: It's important for you to regain your own feeling of personal autonomy and take charge of your own life. Remember, these old wounds were created by others who had authority of some sort, so healing happens when you reassert your own authority and agency in decision-making.

The Gift: The gift of having been exploited by others *in the past* is that once you become aware, as you are now, you learn to develop an improved ability to read people and get a sense of who you can trust. You become more vigilant and highly intuitive. You also, simultaneously, get an important lesson in forgiveness and the main beneficiary of that lesson is you. It becomes critical to learn to forgive yourself when another person has taken advantage of you. Obviously, there's also an incredible opportunity with all of these misbehaviors to learn how to forgive others without seeing it as a sign of weakness after someone has hurt you. It's an opportunity to learn that granting forgiveness is not a gift you give away weakly, but instead that it's actually a precious gift you give yourself because you don't deserve to carry the burden of someone else's misdeeds.

6) Humiliation

This occurs when an individual takes a superior posture and demeans, embarrasses or ridicules another. It's bad enough if it happens privately behind closed doors, but it can be even worse if it occurs in front of others or includes taunts at your expense.

The Effect: Those who have been on the receiving end of behavior designed to humiliate can potentially struggle with the effects for a lifetime. It instills profound feelings of shame that can cause people to surround themselves in silence in order to avoid attention or the limelight.

The Goal: In order to resolve past humiliation, someone who's been victimized needs to restore their resilience to the opinions of others and regain their own personal equilibrium. They need to give more credence to their own good opinions rather than voices in the crowd.

The Gift: The gift of having been humiliated by others *in the past* is that once you become aware, as you are now, you become forced to develop a thicker skin and be more resilient in the face of criticism or taunting. You learn to filter out and reject the non-supportive voices of those who seek to control and demean you. On the other side of humiliation lies the gift of regained *pride* and *confidence* in yourself. When you legitimately don't really care what other people think of you, you have found your own unique kind of super power. How great would life be if you were self-approved and you knew it?!

7) Abandonment

This occurs when you are vulnerable or at risk and another party, who could legitimately be expected to care for you or be involved in your care, just leaves physically, emotionally or spiritually. It doesn't even really matter so much why. The effect can be very similar whether it's a divorce, an addiction or a death. It's all about feeling alone and at risk.

The Effect: Those who've felt abandoned can also struggle a great deal. In addition to the difficulties of getting what they need to survive and thrive, or of finding someone to do that for them, it can wreak havoc on one's ability to trust again. That, in turn, can lead to feelings of rage, anger, disassociation, worthlessness or any number of other reactions.

The Goal: In order to heal abandonment, you'll need to have a deep understanding of your feelings around it and the person you hold responsible. Like all of these misbehaviors, the key will be re-triggering the initial wound and learning that you are okay, that you survived and that you managed to, get everything you needed. Then, from there, learning to forgive and find gratitude in whatever happened will complete the process.

The Gift: The gift of having been abandoned by others *in the past* is that once you become aware, as you are now, you become forced to acknowledge that you made it through as a result of your own grit, determination and will to survive. Plus, it's probably a powerful observation to notice who *did* step forward and make a tremendous difference in your life, especially if they didn't have to do it as a result of a title or position. You have absolutely no control whatsoever over another person's presence or participation in your life and what they did or didn't do has very little, if anything, to do with you. When you understand that people are just doing the best they can with what they have in the moment, it becomes possible to reevaluate some of the thoughts, beliefs, fears and expectations you may have created or developed around what another person did or didn't do and how that related to you. The truth is, sometimes you can have addition through subtraction when you realize that some people are out of your life because they simply brought more value to you by being absent than their presence ever could have created.

8) Violence

This occurs when acts of physical aggression or battery are directed against you that can result in bodily injury or even fearful thoughts. This can also be perpetrated by an assault when just words and threats of violence are enough to trigger fear and intimidation.

The Effect: Those who've been on the receiving end of violent acts or intimidation can react in a number of ways.

Occasionally they can live in fear of bullying acts and manifest post-traumatic stress symptoms. This tends to lead to withdrawing and isolating behaviors as a means of self-defense. Occasionally, the abused can also become the abuser if that behavior has been normalized and violence is seen as a legitimate response to anger.

The Goal: In order to heal victims of violence, there needs to be a recovery of the power that was taken from them. That can happen in a number of ways, but it often requires a tilt of balance in the power dynamic. Whether the victim gets empowered and strengthened in some way or the perpetrator gets weakened through prosecution or some other way, the net effect is achieved by a role reversal or some type of change in perspective.

The Gift: The gift of having been abused violently by others *in the past* is that once you become aware, as you are now, you may decide you have no choice but to grow your own strength in a way that undermines and forever changes the dynamic that left you vulnerable from the beginning. Essentially, there are two types of growth. In *evolutionary growth*, you advance and make new distinctions gradually over time. In *revolutionary growth*, you need to find a way to dig down deep within yourself to find the wherewithal to surmount a challenging scenario. Whatever the impetus, there's something powerful and cathartic about rising to a challenge and growing into a more empowered version of yourself.

9) Isolation

This occurs when those in authority ignore you, don't spend enough time with you or overlook your best interests in some way. Sometimes it can be an overt and willful attempt to isolate and other times, it can simply be an unintended consequence of a work schedule or even an untimely death. In either case, the damage can be painful and potentially debilitating.

The Effect: Those who've been isolated, especially in their formative years, may experience a variety of challenges. Without caring role models or mentors, they may lack the examples they'll need for normal development in areas like trust, communication, bonding, conflict resolution and others.

The Goal: In order to heal the effects of growing up in isolation, it's important to have an empowering story that doesn't lay blame at your own feet. It also requires a willingness and a desire to find others who can stand in and demonstrate the kinds of beliefs, habits and actions of a competent and confident adult. You'll need to learn resilience and develop effective skills and behaviors. It's not so important where you learn them and from whom, it only matters that you learn them.

The Gift: The gift of having been isolated by others *in the past* is that once you become aware, as you are now, you get to become the voice that leads you and the hand that guides you. You are guided by your own soul and desires and you now have an opportunity to seek out all-new mentors that align with your spirit and dreams. You also recognize the blessing that comes from not having to un-do the negative messaging that debilitates so many who did have present role models, even if they were damaging or created psychic wounds with their presence.

10) Objectification

This occurs when people take away your human characteristics and seek to define you in an unflattering or inhuman light. Referring to people as animals, dogs or other negative associations is oftentimes a precursor to abuse or attack because it whittles away inhibitions against violence or other anti-social behavior. It's a lot harder to inflict pain or distress on another human who's likable or familiar to us. But if we can strip them of their very humanity, it becomes easier to mistreat them with impunity.

The Effect: Those who've been objectified for long periods of time, especially when it starts young or is inflicted by someone in a position of authority, tend to struggle with low self-esteem. They literally are at risk of buying into what they've been told for years even if every shred of evidence available conflicts with the abuser's viewpoint.

The Goal: In order to clean up the after-effects of objectification, it's important to get other perspectives that contradict the objectifier and use your own inner voice, and forgiveness for yourself and others, to reclaim your humanity and inherent worth. No matter what you have done or not done, you are still worthy of love and no one else has the right to define you.

The Gift: The gift of having been objectified by others *in the past* is that once you become aware, as you are now, you can empower yourself to reclaim your own humanity. Having this experience will teach you to find the courage to redefine yourself. It will teach you to embrace your humility and learn to appreciate progress over perfection. It will show you how to also begin to forgive yourself and others. These are all profoundly human qualities and you have them. You will know you have them because you've had to reclaim them the hard way. That means you've truly earned them.

11) Rejection

This happens when you're routinely and purposefully made to feel like you're not enough for one reason or another, or even for no reason at all. The net effect is that either love or attention gets taken away punitively. This tends to be a precursor to isolation, and the harm and pain it causes.

The Effect: Those who've felt rejected usually feel less confident in their own inherent worth and value. They also tend to accept and excuse way too much poor treatment while settling for far too little in return just to maintain connection. They tend to over-value any feeling of connection to others even if that person hasn't earned the right to be their friend.

The Goal: The secret to healing from rejection, like most of the misbehaviors we've covered, is in taking back your own self-worth and finding your own tribe where you are celebrated, appreciated and welcomed. It may seem hard if you've never experienced that, but there are good, well-meaning people in the world who offer those experiences simply because it aligns with their deepest values.

The Gift: The gift of having been rejected by others *in the past* is that once you become aware, as you are now, you can reclaim your own self-approval and inherent worth on your terms. You develop a new appreciation for who you are and what you have to offer the world. You decide what you believe and to whom you will listen. You seek out your own truth. You find your own tribe who will get you and resonate with you. You embrace what's great about you and even decide to commit to make some changes if there's something you don't like that's fixable. You've always had this right and ability, even if you didn't know it or exercise the choice. Today is a new day and other people's opinions of you are not binding.

12) Sexual assault

This occurs anytime someone attempts an inappropriate, illegal and indefensible abuse of trust and power for their own sexual gratification when consent is not or cannot be given. It is a violation that has little to do with sex and far more to do with power or force.

The Effect: Those who've been sexually abused in some way can have a range of effects that can vary widely depending on many factors including age, relationship to the perpetrator, use of violence and many more. It can be complex, wide-ranging and occasionally unpredictable in its effects. Beyond the violation of trust involved, it also has a tendency to distort and disrupt an individual's own relationship to a healthy sexuality. For instance, some abuse survivors have been known to embrace promiscuity while others experience a total repulsion to the mere idea of sexual activity. So, the responses can be as varied as the people involved. No matter how the misbehavior manifests or presents, you deserve to be free of its effects.

The Goal: Because sexual abuse can present in so many different ways, it can be somewhat complex to heal its effects, but it is absolutely doable and you deserve to experience it! Some of the main factors in the healing journey would include forgiving yourself for any responsibility you may feel, fairly or unfairly, assigning blame to a perpetrator and holding them accountable. You'll also want to be able to dissolve any shame or blame you may feel so that you can speak your truth about what happened to you with people who've earned the right to hear it and support you. Lastly, if you really want to heal it completely, you will own the fact that you are not what happened to you. When you can somehow find forgiveness for your perpetrator, then you will be totally free, just as you deserve. Let me be clear: that doesn't mean you don't want the perpetrator to take responsibility or be punished. It just means that you choose to no longer let someone else rent space in your head that will only make you feel bad. While I can't possibly cover every single circumstance or scenario in this brief summary, there is no acceptable excuse for sexual abuse. None.

The Gift: The gift of having been sexually abused by others *in the past* is that once you become aware, as you are now, you may decide to separate yourself and who you are at the deepest level from your story or what happened *to* you. By rising above victimization, you can find your own empowerment. While you may have been overpowered in a moment in the past, you can find an all-new level of strength you never knew you had. When your voice was temporarily silenced, you can get it back, stronger and steadier than ever. In deception, you can find truth. Where you may have been held against your will, you can emerge on the other side freer than you've ever felt. It's one thing to be a sexual abuse survivor, it's quite another to make the leap to thriver by taking back the power that was temporarily taken from you.

While it can sometimes seem like we have a long way to go as a society in making this right, I also know that we have come a very long way. If you've been abused in this way, you are very far from alone and when you come forward, you stand with some great and powerful women and men who spoke their truth and broke down walls before you that you won't have to face. By taking back your power after sexual abuse, you literally become one with the force and strength behind you that paved the way for you. As Martin Luther King, Jr. said, "The arc of the moral universe is long, but it bends toward justice." We're still getting there as a society and the one thing that helps us all the most is the sound of an aggrieved, but empowered, voice that simply has the courage and will to say this is not how this story ends.

The Twelve Traumatic M.I.S.B.E.H.A.V.I.O.R.S.

Manipulation
Injustice
Shame
Betrayal
Exploitation
Humiliation
Abandonment
Violence
Isolation
Objectification
Rejection
Sexual assault

Now that you have a new understanding of the 12 Traumatic M.I.S.B.E.H.A.V.I.O.R.S., it will help to actually take this content and turn it into powerful, compelling exercises that will strengthen you. Here's a simple format that can transform you from an awareness to a commitment, and that's where all the power is to set you free and move you forward into the kind of life and love you deserve. Simply use this format and copy it into a journal or fill it out in the *Companion. Peace.* workbook. As you begin to fill in the blanks, you will also begin to find the resolve to find freedom.

If I forever fault _____ for _____,

I would miss out on the following gifts and benefits:

_____

_____

_____

Instead of simply holding a grudge that punishes me, I *choose* to

believe this: _____

_____

_____

And I *commit* to do this: _____

_____

_____

This is the gift I give to myself because I deserve it. It is written. It is resolved. It is done. (Date) _____.

Sample Commitment:

If I forever fault <u>my dad</u> for <u>manipulating me to feel like I was</u> <u>a bad child</u>, I would miss out on the following gifts and benefits:

189

I never would have developed the strength to know for sure that I wasn't bad. I never would have learned to think for myself instead of believing everything I heard. I wouldn't have learned to believe in myself and I might have become a quitter. I never would have become such a good and caring parent. I never would have discovered how good it feels to stand up for what's right! Instead of simply holding a grudge, I choose to believe:

My dad did the best he could with what he knew at the time.

If he had known better, or was raised better himself, he would have done better. Despite it all, I know that he loved me the best way he knew.

And I commit to do this:

I will continue to be the change I wish to see in the world by being understanding, accepting people where they are, loving them without an agenda and I will do my best to model the love and forgiveness I want to feel!

This is the gift I give to myself because I deserve it. It is written. It is resolved. It is done. (Date) _____

Chapter 11:

Knowing and Showing your Value
The 8 F's of Personal Transformation™

Now that we've covered how to heal some major unresolved wounds from childhood, and hopefully made some huge progress, it's time to turn our attention toward growing your own greatness and self-worth. This is a critically important process for a couple of reasons: first, when we change the quality of your thoughts, we simultaneously change the quality of your life because of what we call the Cycle of Success. Here's how that process works:

When you begin to be more conscious of your thoughts and focus in the direction of what you want rather than what you don't want, it begins to positively impact on your **Potential**. That's the first of the four components in the Cycle of Success. It really is kind of simple: better thoughts, better potential. That, alone, is a powerful first step in transforming your life. Then, when you feel better about your potential, you feel more hopeful and you look for what's great instead of what's wrong. So that changes your whole attitude. When you have a better outlook, that leads to the second component in the Cycle of Success which is **Action**. Due to the mental work you've already done to improve your patterns of thinking, when you start to see and feel your potential, you take much better action in the direction of what you want. You go on dates or take action on the things that used to get pushed aside by that old tendency to procrastinate. You start to make those phone calls you were supposed to make and call on new potential customers. You start a business. You take more calculated risks by getting outside your old comfort zone. As a result of being in such a positive state of mind and taking conscious, decisive and strategic action, great things begin to happen so you reap the rewards.

That leads to the third component of the Cycle of Success called **Results**. Once again, it's really simple. Better thoughts. Better potential. Better action. Better results. This is where life really begins to change and I *love* it when I watch my clients hit that sweet spot where everything starts to come together. Great things keep happening and every time that occurs, you hit the fourth level in the Cycle of Success known as **Beliefs**. When you make some changes and continue to see and feel good things happen, it can't help but change your beliefs about what's really possible. It starts to fundamentally change your expectations! You start to believe in yourself. You begin to take on challenges that once seemed overwhelming.

Once you complete the entire cycle from Potential through Action and onto new improved Results and stronger Beliefs, your life is changing in real time. Great things are starting to happen, and miracles are occurring. This is when life gets really good and momentum starts rolling! Every little victory builds upon itself and success begins to magnify. Your energy is magnetic, and you start to notice that the right people and opportunities are being drawn *toward* you at the right time! Those old "closed doors" open wide and possibilities materialize out of nowhere. As long as this Cycle continues, you start to realize that the sky is the limit and success is practically guaranteed.

If that whole Cycle of Success sounds exciting, it is absolutely an incredible ride. However, I would be remiss if I didn't make very clear that this whole Cycle, unfortunately, also works in reverse. You can either spiral upward toward greatness, or you can spiral downward into fear. Anxiety. Shame. Hopelessness. Something tells me, though, that you already know this information, maybe even all too well. The fact is, energy attracts energy, so if you picked up this book with the hope of finally solving your relationship challenges and struggles, you probably know this either very, very well or at least intuitively. While that may sound like bad news, the good news is that in the pages to follow, I am about to share a really powerful way to change this, heal this and get your energy spiraling back upward again. I call this exercise the 8 F's of Personal Transformation.

The 8 F's of Personal Transformation

These eight F words (no, not that one!) I'm about to share represent the eight major sectors or components of a life well-lived. In each of these individual sectors, we both expend energy and receive energy. When an individual area consumes more energy than it provides on a regular basis, it will operate at a deficit and over time, it will deplete you. However, if an area creates more energy than it consumes, you operate at a surplus and the net effect is that you will feel empowered.

The good news is that when at least a majority of those eight areas are collectively operating at surplus and creating more energy than you consume, that's where you begin to experience true happiness. When they're all operating at a surplus, you begin to see, hear, feel and know that your life is on purpose and you experience real satisfaction and joy. You are motivated. You don't dread getting out of bed, you tend to wake up feeling good and ready to go on most days.

When one individual area out of the eight is in deficit mode, it can wear you down over time and lead to struggle, frustration or reduced quality of life. When multiple areas are operating at a deficit over time, your quality of life can take a serious hit and ultimately, it can lead to anxiety, burnout and even depression. The longer this goes on, the more difficult or even debilitating it can become over time.

By separating these areas into different categories, I want to help you identify what sectors of your life are working and creating satisfaction for you now because we always want to focus on what's great first. Then, I want to help you identify where exactly you may be getting stuck or being held back. If you can isolate those areas, we can help you figure out what needs to happen in order to improve things. Now that we understand the assignment, let's identify The 8 F's of Personal Transformation themselves and get started.

Friends

In this important area, the quality of your life is dramatically affected by your social interactions with others. Human beings are, by nature, pack animals and are wired for connection with others, especially those of like mind. In fact, human interaction is so important to overall well-being that the absence of it is actually recognized as a form of torture or extreme punishment. The absence of friendly support is the literal root of extreme wounds like abandonment. Rejection. Loneliness. Shame. Guilt. Likewise, having support is an important antidote to all of the 12 M.I.S.B.E.H.A.V.I.O.R.S. I covered in the previous Chapter. It goes a long way toward repairing the damage caused or avoiding it altogether. Human beings need to be supported for healthy development and even more so when we may be going through a challenging time. That's why it's such a critical indicator of the state of your emotional health and an absolute game-changer when it comes to making a rapid transformation for the better.

Family

On a similar note, family, like friends, is also a huge source of social interaction and human support. For some, it can be a huge benefit if you come from a close, loving or emotionally supportive family. However, if your family is dysfunctional, generally unsupportive or emotionally unhealthy in some way, or even abusive, it can create a huge emptiness that can be challenging, but not impossible, to fill. It's in a healthy, well-adjusted family that the groundwork is laid for a child's lifetime of success.

Likewise, once that child has grown into adulthood, the support of a loving family is a critical component for success through both good and bad times. Whether you're talking blood relatives who've been together for a lifetime or even fast friends who just met, there simply is no substitute for great people who have your back through thick and thin.

Fun

The third component in the 8 F's is oftentimes a by-product of the first two components because friends and family are often the source of, or fellow participants in, the pursuit of Fun. Perhaps you've heard the saying, "All work and no play makes Jack a dull boy." It's absolutely true because we know beyond any doubt whatsoever that having fun may be one of the purest, true drivers of an individual's quality of life. Sometimes it can come in the form of frivolity and lightheartedness. Sometimes it shows up in the form of adventure and escape from routine. Sometimes it's a product of mutually enjoyable activities. However, no matter what form it shows up in, there's no denying the simple necessity, power and game-changing quality of a little well-timed fun.

Focus

The next critical component in an individual's quality of life is their predominant focus or mental clarity. There is incredible power in decisiveness, mental acuity and a clear-eyed vision of who you are, what you want and where you're headed. As they say, knowledge is power, as long as it's applied. The ability to focus on and pursue compelling goals is a precursor to an engaging life, well-lived. Likewise, muddled thinking, a lack of motivation or just plain impotent goals are indicative of a life stalled and going nowhere quickly. That kind of confusion can't possibly drive engagement, excitement or any type of excellence. In fact, it's basically a recipe for staying stuck, because as the saying goes, "When you don't know where you're going, any road will take you there." Bottom line, you can't possibly feel good when you're stuck and spinning your wheels.

Fitness

Another important driver for the quality of your life is your overall level of health and wellness. You can't exactly light the world on fire when you're sick and tired, lacking vigor or generally unwell. Your physical health and strength can either power your deepest dreams or it can sabotage you before you even get started. Without a high level of vitality and personal power, you will struggle and stay stuck. Energy is everything when it comes to taking action and making things happen. That's why your level of personal fitness is such an important predictor of future achievement. If you want to have the wherewithal to make things happen and experience success, you have to be able to have the drive to pursue excellence and harness your best efforts.

Fulfillment

One of the key attributes to achieving true fulfillment is a feeling of alignment with your soul's purpose and meaningful work in the pursuit of compelling goals. Not knowing why you're here and doing work that means nothing can kill your soul or crush your spirit. It really is draining to have to seemingly surrender your dreams and desires in return for a paycheck. No amount of money can make up for the feeling of golden handcuffs holding you back and keeping you stuck but there *are* alternatives. Many people are far more driven by the pursuit of happiness, meaning and contentment than they are by trading their time for money in order to fulfill someone else's dreams. *This* is a total game-changer that makes all the difference when it comes to eliminating frustration and discontent.

Finance

This is yet another huge driver of your personal power and satisfaction in life because it is one of the primary indicators of your literal "value" in this world. One of the greatest sources of pain and frustration in this world is living in poverty, whether it's reflected in your surroundings or in your mindset or consciousness. We've probably all been there at some level when we had bigger desires than bank accounts, but it takes on a whole new meaning when it seems like your very survival is at stake. It is a source of great pain for many who may make the mistake of confusing their net worth with their self-worth. That's why it's so important to be aware of the power and importance of putting your financial house in order.

Faith

This is the eighth and final driver of my 8 F's and I shared it last because it's sometimes looked at as a higher power. While it's not an absolute must for one to pursue spirituality in the pursuit of happiness, it's clear that a relationship to some sort of Grand Organizing Designer (see what I did there?) provides far too many benefits to just overlook it. For many, finding faith in something bigger than themselves, seeking a higher purpose or literally having the "support" of a loving Creator can make all the difference in the world in good times or not so good. Remember how I said how important it is to be supported and loved? Whether it's friends, family, a partner or a Supreme being, we all want to be loved and supported in the way we need it, and we don't do nearly as well when we're seemingly on our own.

Here's Why This Changes *Everything*

Now that you've discovered my 8 F's of Personal Transformation, let me tell you why this matters so much. These eight drivers of personal satisfaction are the individual components, assembled here for the first time ever, that have the power to forever change your life and I'm about to show you why that's not just hyperbole or blowing smoke. Think of it as the literal and specific ingredient list in the recipe for happiness!

Friends
Family
Fun

Focus

Fitness

Fulfillment

Finance

Faith

With these eight individual and simple items, I'm going to show you a number of things that just might blow your mind and change the way you see the world for good. No matter how useful or clever you think this list may look at first glance, you've barely even touched the surface. I have a whole methodology here that will take you deeper, reveal more than you know, and start to rewire your entire mindset for success rather than struggle. Now I know all of that may sound like a pretty tall order but stay with me and I will deliver. This is where things start to get good. Really good.

The 8 F's of Personal Transformation

- These 8 things determine your quality of life every single day.
- These 8 things will show you why, exactly, your quality of life isn't where you want it.
- These 8 things indicate, reveal and pinpoint your exact level of self-worth.
- These 8 things will help you raise your level of self-worth in minutes.
- These 8 things determine who will be attracted to you as a potential partner.

- These 8 things determine who will *not* be attracted to you as a potential partner.

- These 8 things will help you realize why you attract the same wrong partners.

- These 8 things will help you attract a much higher-quality potential partner.

- These 8 things will show you how to change your quality of life in a heartbeat.

- These 8 things will reveal exactly what's missing in your life.

- These 8 things will pinpoint your deepest fears, challenges and pain points.

- These 8 things will show you how to change and heal.

- These 8 things will show you precisely what's already great, so you can have even more gratitude.

- These 8 things will give you a road map to a life you love.

So, Are You Ready to Get Started?

First, I want to ask you some questions. When I deliver on everything I just wrote, are you ready to step up and *do* the work? Are you committed to having the life, the love and the true happiness you claim you want? If your answer is yes, let's get started!

It's time to jump in and get some all-new clarity. If you have my *Companion. Peace.* workbook, I've conveniently printed these questions and exercises in a format that makes following along and doing the work very simple and convenient. Plus, I give you plenty of space to fill in the blanks and organize your answers for easy reference. If you don't have the workbook, pick up a notebook where you can record your answers and do your work. The first step in that process is to go deeper by adding some numbers to those simple letters. In each individual category, ask yourself the following question:

On a scale of 1-10, how am I doing in the area of _____?

The First F: FRIENDS: In our first example regarding the category of Friends, the question is, on a scale of 1-10, how am I doing in the area of Friends? In order to answer that, you'll need to decide on the quality and quantity of the social interaction in your life. Do you have a great collection of friends you count on for support, advice, fun and frivolity? Are they high-quality friends who you respect and appreciate, or are they more acquaintances than friends through the power of proximity? Do your friends have your back through thick and thin? If you really needed help in the middle of the night, is there someone who would answer your call and be there by your side? Do your friends get and support you or do you think they take advantage of you or maybe gossip behind your back? Do they bring out the best in you or do they weaken your resolve and undermine you? Are they loyal? Trustworthy? Are you tolerating more than you should because the bar of your expectations is set far too low? These are just a few questions to consider in order to frame your thinking. Of course, you may have some others that apply to you and your situation only. So, with that in mind and all things considered, what score would you give yourself in the area of Friends?

FRIENDS SCORE: _____ **out of 10**

Notes on final score:

Here's where I'm doing great in the area of Friends:

Here's what I should consider changing:

Random notes/thoughts:

The Second F: FAMILY: In our second example regarding the category of Family, the question is on a scale of 1-10, how am I doing in the area of Family? In order to answer that, you'll need to decide on the quality and quantity of the family support and engagement in your life. Is your family close and connected or is there disfunction, dissension or estrangement? Are they generally loving, protective and want the best for you or are you tolerating family members you can't trust as far as you can throw them? If you really needed help in the middle of the night, would they be there for you? Do they bring out the best in you or do they stress you out, tick you off or betray you? Is there an area where you need to speak your truth, set a boundary and enforce it or even avoid someone altogether? Do you need to do a reset on your expectations? These are just a few questions to consider in order to frame your thinking. Of course, you may have some others that apply to you and your situation only. So, with that in mind and all things considered, what score would you give yourself in the area of Family?

FAMILY SCORE: _____ **out of 10**

Notes on final score:

Here's where I'm doing great in the area of Family:

Here's what I should consider changing:

Random notes/thoughts:

The Third F: FUN: In our third example regarding the category of Fun, the question is on a scale of 1-10, how am I doing in the area of Fun? In order to answer that, you'll need to decide on the quality and quantity of good humor, amusement and simple enjoyment in your life. Do you take time for some occasionally frivolous pursuits simply because they bring you an escape from the routine or mundane? Do you schedule in a sufficient amount of rest and relaxation? Do you make time for pleasant experiences or adventures that stretch and challenge you in productive ways? Do you even *know* what brings you fun and enjoyment or are you way too stressed by a job with huge demands and way too little returns other than a paycheck? These are just a few questions to consider in order to frame your thinking. Of course, you may have some others that apply to you and your situation only. So, with that in mind and all things considered, what score would you give yourself in the area of Fun?

FUN SCORE: _____ **out of 10**
Notes on final score:
Here's where I'm doing great in the area of Fun:

Here's what I should consider changing:

Random notes/thoughts:

The Fourth F: FOCUS: In our fourth example regarding the category of Focus, the question is on a scale of 1-10, how am I doing in the area of Focus or mental acuity? In order to answer that, you'll need to decide on the quality and quantity of the level of clarity you have in your life currently. Are you crystal clear on what you want and don't want in life or in your relationships? Do you know what you consider your 'must-haves' or your 'deal-breakers?' Do you manage your state effectively in order to stay positive and move in the direction you desire or are you clueless about what you want out of life and just drifting? Do you maintain a strong mindset in order to push through challenge or are just kind of aimlessly taking life as it comes with no thought of tomorrow? Do you have compelling goals that inspire you and help you greet each new day with hope and vigor? These are just a few questions to consider in order to frame your thinking. Of course, you may have some others that apply to you and your situation only. So, with that in mind and all things considered, what score would you give yourself in the area of Focus?

FOCUS SCORE: _____ **out of 10**
Notes on final score:
Here's where I'm doing great in the area of Focus:

Here's what I should consider changing:

Random notes/thoughts:

The Fifth F: FITNESS: In our fifth example regarding the category of Fitness, the question is on a scale of 1-10, how am I doing in the area of physical Fitness? In order to answer that, you'll need to decide on the level of your personal health and wellness. Are you in good shape physically, free of pre-existing conditions that limit you? Or do you have some health issues that you know could be reversed with better self-care? Is your weight well within normal guidelines like the BMI index or do you need to perhaps manage it better in some way? Are you getting regular checkups with your doctors and doing preventive maintenance where appropriate? Do you eat healthily and treat your body as a temple rather than a dumpster? Do you maintain a good amount of energy and get adequate sleep, or do you have some changes to consider? These are just a few questions to consider in order to frame your thinking. Of course, you may have some others that apply to you and your situation only. So, with that in mind and all things considered, what score would you give yourself in the area of Fitness?

FITNESS SCORE: _____ **out of 10**

Notes on final score:

Here's where I'm doing great in the area of Fitness:

Here's what I should consider changing:

Random notes/thoughts:

The Sixth F: FULFILLMENT: In our sixth example regarding the category of Fulfillment, the question is on a scale of 1-10, how am I doing in the area of having a mission that Fulfills me? In order to answer that, you'll need to decide whether you feel like you're on purpose, with meaningful work and goals that drive you. Do you wake up looking forward to your day or is every day an exercise in boredom and drudgery? Are you aligned with your ideals and goals and feel like you're making progress in the direction of those dreams? Do you know what you're here for and feel like you're making a difference, or do you just wander aimlessly from day to day with no compelling vision for your future? These are just a few questions to consider in order to frame your thinking. Of course, you may have some others that apply to you and your situation only. So, with that in mind and all things considered, what score would you give yourself in the area of Fulfillment?

FULFILLMENT SCORE: _____ **out of 10**
Notes on final score:
Here's where I'm doing great in the area of Fulfillment:

Here's what I should consider changing:

Random notes/thoughts:

The Seventh F: FINANCE: In our seventh example regarding the category of Finance, the question is on a scale of 1-10, how am I doing in the area of my personal and professional Finances? In order to answer that, you'll need to decide on the status of your current financial situation as well as your future financial picture. Have you been a good steward with your money? Do you have money in the bank or in different vehicles that provide for your future? Are you financially solvent now and do you have a plan to be financially free? Are you able to comfortably afford some key luxuries or does it feel like you live from paycheck to paycheck? Or maybe you're not even earning a paycheck currently?

These are just a few questions to consider in order to frame your thinking. Of course, you may have some others that apply to you and your situation only. So, with that in mind and all things considered, what score would you give yourself in the area of Finance?

FINANCE SCORE: _____ **out of 10**
Notes on final score:
Here's where I'm doing great in the area of Finance:

Here's what I should consider changing:

Random notes/thoughts:

The Eighth F: FAITH: In our eighth example regarding the category of Faith, the question is on a scale of 1-10, how am I doing in the area of Faith and Spirituality? In order to answer that, you'll need to decide what you believe in regard to whether you have a relationship with a higher power. If you do follow a spiritual path, is it where and how you'd like it to be currently? Or if you hold an atheist or agnostic viewpoint, do you feel good about that? Is there anything you feel like you'd want to change or improve? Do you want to be more observant of worship traditions, join a religious community or study the scriptures? Do you want to be more prayerful or commit to a regular meditation practice? If your religion is kindness, do you want to contribute more service toward that end? These are just a few questions to consider in order to frame your thinking. Of course, you may have some others that apply to you and your situation only. So, with that in mind and all things considered, what score would you give yourself in the area of Faith?

FAITH SCORE: _____ **out of 10**
Notes on final score:
Here's where I'm doing great in the area of Faith:

Here's what I should consider changing:

Random notes/thoughts:

Let's See Where You Stand

Now that you've scored yourself in each of the eight areas, we want to go back and add up the total number of points. With a score of 1-10 spread over eight different categories, you have a very wide range of potential scores. If you give yourself only one single point in each category, meaning that things are not good at all and require a great deal of work, you'd have a total of 8 points. On the other hand, if your life is beyond amazing and hits the top of the scale with 10's all the way across the board, you'd have a score of 80 possible points. I suspect a score of either 8 or 80 would be very rare and unlikely because people seldom lead lives where everything is terrible and they seldom lead lives where everything is perfect. We all have challenges and we all have gifts. It's not so much about the total numerical score at the end; it's really about the quality of life that score represents.

Your Total Score in The 8 F's: _____

The Key:

8-30   We have some work to do so let's get started!

31-40   I'm really glad you're doing this exercise. Great things ahead!

41-50   You're in a wonderful position to make some real shifts!

51-60   Good job and we still have some room to grow!

61-70   Tremendous job on a high-quality life!

71-80   This is incredible! Congratulations on a life well-lived!

Now that you have your total, you also have an all-new understanding of where you are in this moment. Remember, whether you love your score, or you think it's low, it is nothing more than a snapshot of a moment in time. The good news is that in the next Chapter, I'm going to walk you through some game-changing exercises that can make a tremendous difference in both your life and in the life of others in your circle.

Chapter 12:

Growing Your Greatness – The 8 F's of Personal Transformation

Now that you know your score, I need to enlighten you about something I mentioned to you in passing in the last Chapter. You may recall that I promised this diagnostic tool would help you understand who will be attracted to you as a potential partner *and* who will *not* be attracted to you as a potential partner. How do I know that and make such a bold claim? It's pretty easy actually and there's a concept you should know.

It's All about Relative Value

In my observation and work with so many couples over the years, I find that most couples who get together and have what it takes to at least be together long term tend to self-select unconsciously based on the concept of Relative Value. In other words, most individuals who do this diagnostic and compare it to their partners will find that their scores are very often within plus or minus five points either way. In a sense, it's an invisible representation and a benchmark of a couple's compatibility, which is a primary assessment made by every dating couple ever.

My plus/minus differential observation is not an absolute rule but it's a valid observation. For instance, if you score a 67 (and that's a pretty solid score), you will most likely find that your partner who matches up with you will probably score themselves somewhere between a 62 and a 72. That's because I estimate that most couples who are successful in partnership together tend to value themselves at a very similar level. It predicts pretty well who may get together, who may stay together and who will probably never get together.

It would be really difficult for a partnership to blossom between someone who rates their score as a 24, for instance, and another partner who rates their score as a 72. That's because the self-worth valuation differential is just too great. Those two scores are literally worlds apart and I suspect, unworkable. Even if they did get together in proximity for some reason, the superior/inferior dynamic would probably be just too great to be sustainable. Basically, one partner would think very poorly of themselves while the other had a very high opinion of their own value. I suspect one partner would be constantly propping up the other's self-esteem and they'd grow increasingly irritated with their perceived neediness. Meanwhile, the other partner would vacillate between relying on the support and being threatened by it at the same time. They'd also probably be put off by their partner's seemingly superior posture, which was ironically the thing that probably brought them together in the first place. This would almost certainly lead to resentment on both sides. Even though I'm making a lot of predictions in my fictitious example, it's not a huge stretch. These are commonly observed patterns in relationship dynamics.

There's another reason why partners with similar worths attract each other. It's because the one thing both masculine and feminine partners tend to be attracted to is confidence. While we tend to seek out very different things when it comes to attraction, the one thing we can all agree upon is that we both want to be able to look at our partner and think to ourselves, "Wow, look at my partner; I definitely got the better part of that deal!" Obviously, this is a relative observation based on the individuals involved. For instance, someone who rates themselves a 70 and someone who rates themselves a 50 would be spending their time in different dating pools. They may even have a date or two from a different pool due to one aspect of attraction or another, like good looks, but the odds of a long-term successful and healthy partnership are somewhat remote.

Now that you understand this, you may be wondering, what is the point of all this information and what you can do with it? I'm glad you asked. You may have overlooked it in reading through, but the title of this Chapter is "Growing Your Greatness." I didn't present this self-assessment to you because it's a static, unchangeable number that belongs on your "permanent record." It's not an oil painting that will forever mark your place in time. It's more of a digital snapshot of a single moment in time. It is changeable. But don't get me wrong, most people do tend to stay rather static because they don't do personal development. It might be only 3 or 4 percent of people who ever crack a book, listen to audios or attend a seminar. They don't even realize that change is an option, so they stay stuck. However, *you* undoubtedly do know what's possible and that gives you a tremendous advantage.

Remember those promises I made you earlier about the awesome power of these 8 things? Now that you know what the 8 F's are, let's double back and I'll explain specifically why I wasn't speaking in hyperbole or fluff. When you are aware of the 8 F's, you start to realize how they influence the quality of life every single day. You literally *see* the gap in why your life isn't the way you want it when you realize, for instance, that your finances are a 9 but your health is a 3. It doesn't take a rocket scientist to figure out what's missing or why your self-worth is at the level it's at currently. Now that you've seen your scores in each area, there's also no way you can be unaware of your deepest fears, challenges and pain points. Plus, you can also see at a glance what's working best in your life and where you can find even more gratitude.

With that being said, my 8 F's model isn't just about focusing on what's wrong and holding you back, *far from it.* The real beauty of this model is that it literally shows you where to dig in order to repair the problem. It's also kind of like an x-ray; it shows you what you don't readily see so you know exactly where to focus your efforts and healing attention. One glance at the numbers will give you all you need to know in order to have a road map to a life you love. Once I show you the rest of my process, you'll realize that you can literally create a massive change in the way you feel in minutes! Lastly, these 8 F's are about to help you

Same Sh*t. Different Date.

attract a much higher-quality potential partner because you've been doing your work to earn one!

The Next Step

This is where it starts to get *really* good because the transformation begins to happen organically, and you can seriously feel it changing your state as it occurs. You'll feel yourself start to smile because you now know precisely what used to hold you back and it no longer seems like such a big, overwhelming obstacle. Your back straightens and you feel more grounded and solid in your new decisions. Your shoulders go back slightly and your posture improves as you assume a much stronger physiology of grit, resolve and determination. All in all, this level of clarity and conviction really starts to create a remarkable shift in both your psychology and your physiology. You stand taller. Feel prouder. And you feel more confident that change is not only possible but a must.

Let's use a real-life and real LIVE demonstration that I did at a speaking appearance in Chicago not too long ago as an example. I want to use a strong, personal example because I think you'll get the structure of what I'm doing even faster and to be honest, the human component of my story adds another level of meaning and inspiration to it. When I say 'real-*live*', I mean it happened in front of a room full of people in real time. They witnessed the transformation and in the comments I heard afterward, they didn't just see it, they *felt* it, too. They didn't just feel what *they* felt, either. They specifically felt what my volunteer was feeling as they witnessed the changes in her. It was the crowd's empathy that helped her reluctantly step up for help, even though she didn't fully grasp that was what was happening. I had simply asked the crowd to do a very similar version of this exercise. When I asked who would be willing to share their scores, a bunch of people volunteered. When I asked which area their high score was in and how did they rate it, I had a lot more hands go up to volunteer and answer. Then, when I asked which area was your lowest, and what was your score, this same woman volunteered her score again, as did the man sitting next to her. I only mention the proximity because I didn't know at that moment that the man sitting next to her was actually her husband. I started to figure it out because as I was asking the question to identify the area of struggle, they both revealed the same area: Finance. That was clue number one. I actually asked him first and while I can't swear that I remember the exact numbers, I seem to recall that his lowest number was maybe a six in the area of Finance. Then when I called on the woman next to him, she said her lowest ranking was also in the area of Finance but she gave it a three. This was the exact moment when the plot thickened because they looked at each other with shock. That's when it started to dawn on me, and I suspect a few others who didn't know them, that they were a couple.

Now, as a quick aside for a teachable moment, this is a perfect example of the difference between the way masculine and feminine both process the same situation or scenario. These two people were married. His financial position was the same as hers and vice versa. There was no difference. The numbers, the situation, the household were identical. So how do you explain the discrepancy where he rated the exact same situation twice as good as she did?!? They were both behind in bills. They both

217

recognized finances as their biggest challenge. Yet, somehow, he felt the situation was two times better than she did. The explanation for that is that he was weighing the situation in his masculine brain wired for logic, analysis, single-focus, taking action and blasting through challenge in order to compete and win. She, on the other hand, was navigating the identical scenario in her feminine brain which is wired for feelings and emotion, a need to be safe at all costs and a desire to be protected. Can you now see why they rated the exact same position so very differently?

Back to our story as it unfolded. As she confessed her fear and insecurity publicly, her husband looked at her with the most beautiful combination of empathy for her vulnerability and shock. He had no earthly clue that she was as stressed by things as she confided, but he responded really well with sensitivity and reassurance that things would be okay. Of course, it couldn't have been easy to make that public confession in a room full of people, many they probably knew socially because it was a group that meets monthly. I felt her shame, nervousness and extreme vulnerability as we talked through it publicly. Plus, her sense of reticence was palpable when I asked her if I could work with her right there and then. To her credit, she said yes. As I'm sharing this, keep in mind that you will soon replicate this exact same process in order to make a huge difference for you.

Once we identified her lowest scoring area out of the 8 F's, which as we said in this case was Finances, I explained to her that we always want to look for the low hanging fruit first because that's obviously where the biggest turnarounds are possible. So, I asked her, "What are maybe 3 things you can commit to right now that would help improve the area of finances for you?" As she was thinking to herself, I mentioned that I wanted to acknowledge her for her vulnerability in sharing that not only publicly but with her husband also, who was very reassuring.

Then I said to her, "Now that you've acknowledged the problem and gotten loving support from your husband, how do you feel about the challenge now? Do you feel better or worse?" She thought for a second, looked at her husband, smiled and said, "Yes." I replied, "Great. That's one down, two more to go. Just simply acknowledging how you feel, speaking your truth and sharing it with your husband is *huge,* so that's a massive step in the right direction. So, what ELSE could you do to improve this situation somehow?" As she was thinking, I asked her another question, "Now that you know you and your husband are on the same page about fixing things, and he has been so good about understanding where you were, do you think it would help to sit down and discuss a new spending budget with the goal of eliminating some debt?" She thought for a second and then nodded affirmatively. So, I asked again, "Knowing that you've already shared with your husband and gotten his support in creating a plan, what is one more thing you could commit to doing that will in some way, form or fashion, improve your situation?"

After some further discussion about next steps, we identified that she could have a choice to do one of three things after they researched their situation further. Option number one was she could choose to pay off one smaller bill and apply that payment to a different bill to retire the next bill even faster. Option two was that she could just find one monthly expense they already had and cancel it. Option three was that she could find one area where they were spending regularly and simply choose to give up that expense in order to save the money they were spending. Option three was based on the so-called "Latte Factor" which points out how a $4 latte adds up to a $120 monthly expense which can be better used to invest or pay off debt.

So, in about five minutes in a roomful of people on a sunny, Saturday afternoon, we arrived at the following solutions that had the power to change everything:

1) Share this problem with my husband and ask for support.
2) Look at finances and commit to set up a budget with husband to eliminate debt.
3) Commit to paying off or canceling one monthly bill or eliminating one expense.

That sounds fairly simple and doable, right? Then I asked my final questions: "Okay, now that you've already shared with your husband and gotten his support in creating a plan with you, and you've committed to either pay off one bill, or cancel one monthly bill, or eliminate one expense in order to save that money, how much better do you feel about your finances now?"

The big smile on her face, the relaxed body language, her head on her husband's shoulder and his arm around her said it all. You could see and feel the relief when she said she felt *a lot* better.

At that point, I only had one last question. "Okay, so with those changes in mind, and those changes only, how do you feel about your finances now, on a scale of 1-10?" Her answer might shock you because she said a seven which was a full point higher than her husband rated their financial picture just minutes earlier!

Remember, she had just said she rated her finances a three and designated it as her greatest area of pain moments earlier!

So, I asked her, already knowing the answer, "Hold on, five minutes ago this was your biggest challenge in life! It caused you so much pain that you rated it a three out of 10 points! Now, with one quick chat and a look at some possible situations, you *more than doubled* the way you felt about it. In fact, you feel better about it now than your husband did. And yet, *you haven't actually paid off a single dollar of your debt yet!* How do you explain the fact that you feel twice as good about your biggest problem in minutes?!!"

While I don't remember her exact words, her answer boiled down to this: she felt *safer* because her husband got it and was on board with her so she didn't feel all alone in her worry. She felt *supported* by his commitment with her. And this one is *huge*, even though it wasn't yet fixed, she felt like she had a *workable plan.*

This is perhaps one of the most important lessons in the book and in life. It's not so much about the situation or problem you're facing. It's more so about *the way you feel about* the situation or problem you're facing! As you just saw, we were able to shift that in just minutes!

Now for her, Finance was just one area out of the 8 F's. I encourage you to go back and do this process in all eight areas assuming you didn't give yourself a 10 in all areas, and honestly, most people don't rate themselves as a 10. In fact, in my way of thinking, I think nines across the board might be the best possible score because we always want to have high standards, push to achieve and still have room for improvement. (By the way, that means an awesome score would be a nine in eight different categories or a 72. So, you may want to recalibrate your expectations if you're feeling bad about not getting an 80, which is technically a "perfect score" even though no one is perfect.) In the example I just shared, I honestly don't recall her scores any more, but let's say she had a total score of 59 points when we first added up her results, which according to the key, was at the top of the "good" scale. By simply adding on the additional four points she recaptured in that single area, that five-minute change moved her up to a 63, which puts her solidly in what the key classified as a tremendous job on a high-quality life! That's a pretty huge change! I want you to remember one other thing: if she did the same process in all eight categories, who knows how many points she could recapture? She got four points in one area alone. Even if she only came up with a few things to improve in each area and shifted her score by one in each area, that's a total of eight points or nearly a whole category's worth of points which could move her from good to great! If you start adding up multi-point shifts in a variety of areas, your point differential really starts to increase! It is possible to have a pretty huge before and after shift if you go through the process I just outlined.

The "point" is, your point total is not static and stuck in time. It is possible to be "upwardly mobile" when you focus on what you want, tell the truth about it, get some support and even begin to take some action to change things. That means big changes are very possible with just a little committed *intent.* That's easy! Then when it turns into committed action, it tends to go up again! Then when you see results from your action, it continues even higher! That's when all-new possibilities come into view. However, that's not even the best part of doing this process.

222

The REAL Benefit to This Process

Here's the real beauty of this mechanism I've shared with you. If you recall back before I introduced the 8 F's of Personal Transformation, I claimed one of the big benefits was that it could help you attract a much higher-quality potential partner. You may also recall that I wrote earlier that most people tend to attract and resonate with partners who match them on this diagnostic tool at a rate of plus or minus five. What that means is that once we raise your vibration and your value, you will now have the ability to attract and keep an even higher quality partner. Let me demonstrate specifically what I mean and how that works.

If you consider my plus or minus five differential, someone who values themselves at a level of 65 will be a great match with someone else who rates themselves somewhere between a 60 and a 70. These numbers all represent a very high-quality individual so you can't lose. But watch this to see how it makes a huge difference. If the same person I'm using as an example first scored a 55 before they used my process to raise their score to a 65, that means they may only meet and match with someone who rates as high as a 60 if they don't do the work to improve their value. The difference between a 60 and a 70 is quite large indeed. Imagine dating partners who are obviously confident and know who they are and what they offer. Think about dating someone you'd describe as vibrant and charismatic. A 10-15-point swing in rating is huge when you consider the caliber of partner you can attract. But it's not such a stretch for *you* to step up and do the work to raise your value 10-15 rating points.

Doing your own work on my process literally and figuratively gives you entry into a whole different league. That means that people you once thought couldn't possibly be attracted to you will now find you more compelling and interesting. That means you may approach or chat with people you might not have had the courage to speak with before you did the work. That means you could attract a partner like you who has also handled their own issues. It means you won't have to sit and watch other people who have the kind of partner you'd like to have. You won't have to feel jealous about the relationships other people have. You won't have to struggle with your FOMO-based worries about the Fear of Missing Out. That's because changing your life is now completely in *your* hands.

You Have the Power!

You now have the awareness you need about the deepest, hidden wounds that used to hold you back. You now have the tools and exercises to bring those things into view. You now have the leverage to make change a 'must' so you don't have to feel the pain of staying stuck. You now have the ability to literally create all-new possibilities. You have someone who believes in you, cares about you and wants the best for you: you! Plus, you can add me to that list as well because I don't have to know you to want the best for you. You also have access to me if you want to go deeper and have a guide on this journey to help you push through if you get stuck.

With all of those things I've now given you, I have to admit, there is one thing I have not given you and you do not have. You have all the tools, awareness, drive and skills you need to create some huge positive change in your life and those around you. The one thing you don't have any longer is an excuse about why you can't do this work or have the things you want in your life. It's all here for the taking.

As you complete the assignment in this chapter to "grow your greatness," I've created a list of high-quality questions designed to prompt some great thoughts to help you strategically maximize your score in a way that's organic and authentic. We're talking about your relative value here, so as you improve your own confidence and clarity, you will improve the quality of the partner you can attract and keep. You'll find those questions conveniently assembled in the Appendix at the back of the book for easy referral as you complete the assignment. You'll also find these quality questions listed in my *Companion. Peace.* workbook that was specifically created to facilitate doing this work in one neat and organized format. However you decide to complete the assignment, I'm confident that the rewards you'll reap will be a direct reflection of the effort you make toward doing this healing work.

Chapter 13:

The Past May Predict Your Future, But It's Not Predetermined

First of all, you are amazing and I want to acknowledge you for making it to the final chapter. Some people talk about wanting more love or a better quality of life, but they aren't willing to do the work or commit to what it takes. Because you read this book and did the exercises, you are well on your way. Even if nothing else comes from this book, I truly hope you'll take away one revolutionary and game-changing thought. Those things that you may have thought were hurtful evidence of what was wrong with you and why you weren't worthy of love, weren't happening to torture you. They were happening to *teach* you. They weren't occurring so you would doubt your greatness or give up hope. They were, literally, the exact antidote that was needed for you to find the strength to claim your real self-worth and push against the negative thoughts and fears that were keeping you stuck. When you start to take that in and see it from that perspective, everything begins to change and all new possibilities are created in a moment.

While that realization, alone, may be an even bigger breakthrough than you expected, that is just the beginning. I've packed this book full of both revolutionary awareness's and real, practical tools designed to facilitate and deepen your understandings. I've literally handed you a treasure map with an "X" that marks the spot where you need to dig. In fact, if you read between the lines in my specifically chosen examples and case studies from past clients, you may notice that I practically took the shovel out of your hands and dug *for you*. That's because I am that committed to having you get this breakthrough and the accompanying love that goes with it.

In Chapter 1, I helped you see that the invisible feelings of attraction that get stirred up when you meet someone intriguing may be more about an unconscious longing to complete your unfinished business from childhood than a hormone-fueled desire.

In Chapter 2, I showed you that issues related to your Relationship Origin of Trauma contribute to Continuous Or Recurring Experiences that are designed to bring your attention to areas still in need of healing. This was not a process of punishment, as it may seem, but a benevolent beacon meant to indicate an area for healing you for your highest and best good.

In Chapter 3, I made clear that this cycle of disappointment has never been "personal" and it's actually an expected part of the process of learning and restoration. In fact, when you accept the idea that being triggered by new manifestations of old unresolved wounds is actually the linchpin of the necessary healing process, it's easier to welcome the learning rather than curse it.

In Chapter 4, I set the table for you to look slightly beyond the concept of a soul mate because the automatic presupposition that comes with that word is that you're entering a lifetime contract to be renewed in perpetuity. I believe that sets up an unfair and premature expectation. When you embrace the term "soul messenger" instead, it can keep you focused more on what you're building in the present. It will also help you see the gift in the experience if that relationship doesn't have what it takes to go the distance.

In Chapter 5, I introduce the concept of The Magical Morphing Messenger in order to prepare you for the fact that occasionally, relationships run their course prematurely. That's not necessarily an indictment of you or what you have to offer. It's just a recognition, in advance, that sometimes people come into your life for a reason or season only, and they were never meant to be lifetime partners.

In Chapter 6, I helped you uncover some potential wounds that may have been stealthily hiding in plain sight because you may not have seen the relationship between unique events. While you may have overlooked some very foundational concerns, my unique diagnostic tool helped you identify and root out some serious patterns of Abuse, Bullying, Chaos, Dysfunction or even Environmental issues.

In Chapter 7, I shared with you the concept of the Soul Messenger Matrix and I gave you a simple assessment tool that could help identify some of those deeply foundational wounds and issues that still require some attention and healing. By using my simple H.E.A.R.T. Assessment, you were able to reveal any unfinished business that might attract further ongoing issues.

In Chapter 8, I revealed what it all meant and some of the multiple ways you may be self-sabotaging your relationships. By shining a light on your own personal recipe for disaster in such stark terms, you got to see firsthand why so many of your past relationships may have left you with a bad taste in your mouth. In addition, I shared a specific technique for consciously turning around this totally unproductive pattern.

In Chapter 9, we continued to stack resources to help you make changes and stay on track while building momentum. Once you make a powerful change, it's important to create conditions that *support* that change. Otherwise your risk of falling back into old patterns is high. It's not enough to change your beliefs; you have to change your behavior. You can't just change the meaning; you have to change your mindset. That's why I had you associate your new changes to a powerful new identity supported by your Aspirations. Plus, I had you get crystal clear on the Benefits of changing versus the Costs of not changing. Taken together, these three factors link pain and pleasure to powerful new possibilities.

Once we started to create some new empowering shifts in mindset, I gave you some new tools for a healing transformation in Chapter 10. This is where I introduced my 12 Traumatic M.I.S.B.E.H.A.V.I.O.R.S.™ and the damage that the "dirty dozen" can inflict on innocent people. I truly hope this tool helps provide you with some new empowering alternatives. The fact is, you did nothing to deserve what happened to you. If anything, you *deserve* to be free, healed and loved for who you are, as you are, no exceptions.

Then, in Chapter 11, you saw the correlation between your perceived quality of life and your perceived value. I introduced a tool called the 8 F's of Personal Transformation. Once you see at a glance what's working for you, and what's working against you, it helps create an instantaneous shift.

As they say, perception *is* reality so in Chapter 12, I gave you a tool that viscerally helps you shift your perception using small, incremental shifts in your reality. People get stuck in overwhelm and do nothing when they have no idea what to change or how to change. This process makes positive change almost inevitable due to its laser-focused emphasis on small, measurable changes that are simultaneously doable and provable. If you want to change your behavior going forward into the future, the best way to do it is by creating an incentive plan that gives you credit for recognizing the need or desire to change and also acknowledges both the incremental rewards along the path of progress and the even bigger rewards upon reaching those bigger benchmarks. My strategy helps keep you on track because it simultaneously rewards the baby steps AND the giant steps. That's the difference that keeps you moving forward.

The one thing, the only thing, that determines your fate is *you* and you are a product of the thoughts you think on a regular basis. It's not what happened to you. It's not what other people did or didn't do to you. It's ultimately all about you and it always has been.

How else do you explain people who have been through horrific experiences and found a way to bounce back through grit, determination and maybe even forgiveness? Yet at the same time, there are some people who face a relatively minor setback and collapse like a house of cards? The quality of your life is a direct reflection of your dominant thoughts, expectations, beliefs and actions which are, in turn, limited by your doubts, fears and insecurities. No matter what happened or didn't, it ultimately came to serve you in some way and it's your job to figure out how and why with an open heart and mind. When you do the healing work to mitigate your past instead of litigate it, you will know peace. If you can look back over your past with an attitude of gratitude for it all and less judgment and blame for yourself or others, you'll be well on your way to both a life very well-lived and with any luck at all, your very own Legendary Love For Life. I truly hope you'll use this book to create an amazing quality of life with an incredible, loving partner. Love is your birthright and you are more than worthy of having it. You matter. You are enough. You are loved.

I know I've given you a number of writing exercises in this book, but I can't resist the urge to give you just one last assignment. When you DO use this book to create magnificent, lasting change in your life, please write to me and share your success story with me at dave@legendaryloveforlife.com. Simply put, that's why I do this. I'm here to create more love in the world, one person or couple at a time and I'd love to have you join me as a part of that mission. Wishing you all the love, health and happiness you so richly deserve, always.

Same Sh*t. Different Date.

Appendix

Sample questions to help you improve in each area of The 8 F's.

Friends

- Is there someone in your life now who needs to be limited or removed?

- Is there someone who needs to be back in your life (assuming it's possible)?

- Is there a type of person you need to attract into your life?

- Is there something you need to do to meet new friends?

- Is there something you need to stop doing in order to attract the type of friends you desire?

- Who would you need to be in order to attract the type of friends you desire?

- What will you commit to do in order to attract the type of friends you desire?

- Where can you find the types of friends you aspire to know?

- Who else could use a friend like you?

- What can you offer to create a win/win scenario for someone who may be able to help you experience more friendship?

- Is there a friendship you need to clean up by saying something?
- Is there anyone you need to forgive for what they've done or undone?
- Is there a boundary you need to set and enforce?

Family

- Is there someone in your family now who needs to be limited or removed?
- Is there a family member who needs to be back in your life (assuming it's possible)?
- Is there someone in your family you need to call or see more often?
- Is there someone in your family you need to schedule gatherings with more often?
- Do you possibly need to relocate to improve your family relationships?
- Is there something you need to stop doing in order to create more peace in your family?
- Who would you need to be in order to have the kind of family you desire?
- What will you commit to do in order to have the kind of family you desire?
- What can you offer to someone in your family that could make a big difference?
- Is there a family relationship you need to clean up by saying something?

- Is there anyone you need to forgive for what they've done or undone?
- Is there a boundary you need to set and enforce?

Fun

- Is there someone fun you need to call or see more often?
- Is there someone fun you need to schedule gatherings with more often?
- Is there something fun that you enjoy that you need to schedule more often?
- Is there something fun that you might like to try or experience?
- Is there someone who robs you of fun who needs to be limited or removed?
- Is there a type of fun person you need to attract into your life?
- Is there something you need to do to meet new fun friends?
- Is there something you need to stop doing in order to have more fun?
- Who would you need to be in order to attract the type of fun you desire?
- What will you commit to do in order to attract the type of fun you desire?
- Where can you find the type of fun you desire?
- Who else might enjoy committing to having more fun with you?

- What can you offer to create a win/win scenario for someone who may be able to help you experience more fun?

Focus

- Is there something you need get much more clarity on?
- Is there something you need to schedule right now to have more focus?
- Is there something you need to schedule more often?
- Is there someone that robs you of clarity that needs to be limited or removed?
- Is there something that robs you of clarity that needs to be limited or removed?
- Is there something you need to decide right now and commit to doing to have more focus?
- Is there something you know you need to do to be more focused but aren't doing?
- Is there something you need to stop doing in order to get clear and motivated?
- Who would you need to be in order to make massive progress on focus?
- What will you commit to do in order to get clarity and make massive progress?
- Do you need to find a mentor or coach to help you get clarity?
- Who else has done what you'd like to do and how can you learn from them?

- What can you offer to create a win/win scenario for someone who may be able to help you to be more focused?

Fitness

- Is there something you need to do to get more fit?
- Is there something you need to stop doing to get more fit?
- Is there something you need to schedule to get more fit right now?
- Is there something you need to schedule more often to get more fit?
- Is there someone that sabotages your fitness that needs to be limited or removed?
- Is there something that sabotages your fitness that needs to be limited or removed?
- Is there something you need to decide right now and commit to doing to be more fit?
- Is there something you can do right now to get fit but aren't doing?
- Who would you need to be in order to get in great shape and stay that way?
- What will you commit to do in order to get in great shape and stay that way?
- Do you need to find a mentor, trainer or coach to help you get fit?
- Is there a product that can assist you in gaining health and fitness?

- Who else has the fitness you want and how can you learn from them?
- What can you offer to create a win/win scenario for someone who may be able to help you improve your fitness?

Fulfillment

- Is there something you need to do to fulfill your purpose or mission?
- Is there something you need to schedule right now to feel more on purpose?
- Is there something you need to schedule more often to align with your mission?
- Do you need to change your career to find or stay on purpose?
- Is there someone who takes you off-purpose and needs to be limited or removed?
- Is there something that takes you off-purpose and needs to be limited or removed?
- Is there something you need to decide right now and commit to doing in order to increase your level of fulfillment?
- Is there something you know you need to do but aren't doing to be fulfilled?
- Is there something you need to stop doing in order to get on purpose?

- Who would you need to be in order to accomplish your mission?
- What will you commit to do in order to accomplish your mission?
- Do you need to find a mentor or coach to help you get on purpose?
- Who else has done what you'd like to do and how can you learn from them?
- What can you offer to create a win/win scenario for someone who may be able to help you experience more fulfillment in your mission?

Finance

- Is there something you need to do to improve your finances?
- Is there something you need to schedule right now to improve your finances?
- Is there something you need to schedule more often to improve your finances?
- Do you need to change your career to improve your finances?
- Is there someone who sabotages your finances and needs to be limited or removed?
- Is there something that sabotages your finances and needs to be limited or removed?
- Is there a financial habit you need to decide right now and commit to doing?

- Is there something you need to learn about finances that could help change everything?
- Is there something you need to stop doing in order to be financially free?
- Who would you need to be in order to be financially free?
- What will you commit to do in order to be financially free?
- Do you need to find a mentor or coach to help you get financially free?
- Who else has done what you'd like to do financially and how can you learn from them?
- What can you offer to create a win/win scenario for someone who may be able to help you experience more financial progress?

Faith

- Is there something you need to do to improve your faith or spirituality?
- Is there something you need to schedule right now to improve your faith?
- Is there something you need to schedule more often to improve your spirituality?
- Do you need to change your career to align with your spiritual beliefs?
- Is there someone who sabotages your faith and needs to be limited or removed?

- Is there something that sabotages your faith and needs to be limited or removed?

- Is there a spiritual practice you need to decide right now and commit to doing?

- Is there something you know you need to do spiritually but aren't doing?

- Is there something you need to stop doing in order to honor your faith?

- Who would you need to be in order to embody your beliefs and faith?

- What will you commit to do in order to embody your beliefs and faith?

- Do you need to find a mentor or preacher to help you grow your faith?

- Who else embodies your spiritual beliefs and how can you learn from them?

- What can you offer to create a win/win scenario for someone who may be able to help you experience more spirituality?

Same Sh*t. Different Date.

About the Author:

Dave Elliott

When it comes to making sense of the often-mystifying topic of relationships, Dave Elliott is an international relationship coach who breaks down complex concepts into easily understandable principles and practices. Whether he's working one-on-one with a client, being interviewed by the media, writing an article that goes viral on the Internet or creating another relationship book or product, his advice is right on target because he tells it like it is and breaks it down in simple terms.

In his latest book, *Same Sh*t. Different Date.*, Dave uses that gift and ability to simplify the complex and bring the invisible to light in order to promote massive, life-changing healing for all who seek it. This book distills more than a decade of experience and education and multiple tens of thousands of hours spent working directly with, or on behalf of, thousands of clients and individuals into a methodology that will help them heal the lingering wounds that get in the way of them creating the life and love they deserve. This book is a culmination of what is now his life's work and a defining moment in a career dedicated to creating more love, peace and understanding in the world. It is not an overstatement to say this book is a profoundly powerful game-changer and a proud representation of Dave's legacy and mission.

Dave is known for getting results with a variety of techniques that enable rapid transformational change. With his experience and training, he helps teach others how to effectively understand, predict and even influence human behavior. Dave's main focus is helping people navigate the uncertainties of their most intimate relationships. His specialty is helping women learn to understand men and work with them much more effectively in order to bring out the very best in them rather than suffering through the worst from them. Plus, as a neuro-strategist, he provides people with the awareness and specific strategies for success that they need in order to create success.

After his own marriage ended in a painful and disappointing divorce, Dave used that experience to drive him to discover just what it takes to create 'A Legendary Love for Life,' which is, coincidentally, the name of his coaching business. After researching and learning about everything he could find in the field of human relationships, he took the very best information he found and perfected it to make it easier to learn, more memorable and even more effective.

The good news is that on his journey, he met and married a woman who shared his commitment to mastering the area of relationships. Today, he and his wife, Katrina, share a mission to travel the world to touch, move and inspire others in healing their own wounds and forming more conscious, loving and evolved relationships. Together, they look forward to perhaps meeting you at an upcoming seminar or presentation.

In addition to sharing his expertise on TV, on radio, live on stage and as a highly sought-after expert blogger on popular relationship Web sites, Dave has also created and markets his own personal line of products.

His first book, *The Catch Your Match Formula™*, was inspired by the fact that Dave saw too many good people struggle in their dating lives because they were having trouble standing out from the crowd and connecting deeply with other singles. As a result, he set out to write a book that would give people a smart, real-world and no-nonsense approach to building rapport both online and in person. His background in coaching and as an award-winning advertising copywriter was filled with a whole toolbox of professional-quality tools that could be taught easily and effectively in order to make a huge difference quickly and end their struggle. Today, years later, there are many real-world couples who met, got engaged and even married after using the strategies Dave shared in that book. He also has dozens of clients who have used his help to meet their fiancé's and husbands and have become proud members of what is affectionately known as his Very Satisfied Client Club.™

His rapid relationship turnaround CD, known as *The H.U.G. & K.I.S.S. Hierarchy*, will help you elicit and unlock your partner's – or your own – exact love and attraction strategy. This technique is incredibly powerful and transformational because it gives you the exact combination that will open your partner's heart any and every time, so they feel loved in exactly the way they NEED to be loved.

In addition, he's also the Creator of The Man Magnetics Formula™ – a free Web site that teaches women the nine secrets to bring out the very best in men so they can avoid settling for the worst. You can learn all about it and watch hours of free video instruction at www.manmagnetics.com.

Currently, Dave and his wife, Katrina, are back in Dave's hometown of Baltimore, Maryland in the United States but they will also be returning to their other home in Australia. When they're not traveling, teaching or coaching, they're usually renovating a house, investing in properties or spending time with their friends and family, including their amazing grandson, nephew and niece whom they adore.

Made in the USA
Middletown, DE
03 August 2019